SURVIVING THE CRASH

Finding Inner Peace Through Forgiveness

Krystal!! Thank you so much for your support!! Hugs!!

Bulk purchase discounts and customized copies are available by contacting the author at https://survivingthecrash.co/

978-1-7774219-1-5

This book was published with the support of Happful.com

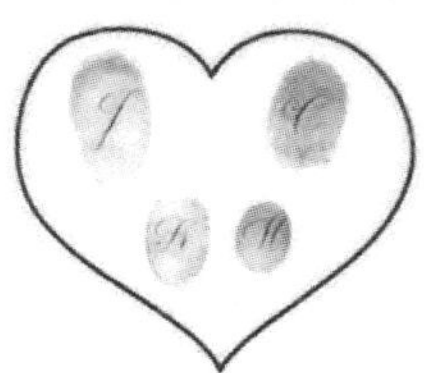

To everything there is a season,
and a time to every purpose
under the heaven;
a time to be born, and a time to die;
a time to plant, and a time to pluck up
that which is planted;
a time to kill, and a time to heal,
a time to break down,
and a time to build up;
a time to weep, and a time to laugh,
a time to mourn, and a time to dance;
a time to cast away stones,
and a time to gather stones together;
a time to embrace,
and a time to refrain from embracing;
a time to get, and a time to lose;
a time to keep,
and a time to cast away;
a time to rend, and a time to sew;
a time to keep silence,
and a time to speak;
a time to love, and a time to hate;
a time of war
and a time of peace.

Ecclesiastes 3:1-8

DEDICATION

This book is dedicated to the Van de Vorst family who were taken from us far too soon. Chanda, Jordan, Kamryn, and Miguire have filled me with life's most treasured memories as well as the greatest lessons, and for that I am forever grateful!

ABOUT THE AUTHOR

Chad Mierau grew up on his family farm in Saskatchewan, Canada where he learned his strong work ethic and family values. He went on to become a mechanic and a Potash miner, for ten years each, before becoming an entrepreneur. Currently Chad is running five businesses and experiencing his life to the fullest.

Chad has two teenage boys nearing the end of high school alongside four bonus children with his fiancé, Angie. Residing half of the time in Watrous and the other half in Saskatoon allows him to spend as much time as possible with all six children.

At the time of writing this book, 5 years have passed since losing his sister, brother-in-law, and their 2 beautiful children to a tragic accident involving a drunk driver. In such a short time, life presented Chad with seemingly insurmountable challenges.

After embarking on a personal development journey, many blessings and opportunities started to arrive in his life. Chad has evolved and grown into a sought-after coach and mentor for others experiencing grief, trauma, and relationship concerns. He is extremely grateful to have found his life purpose and to be able to serve others daily. He would not go back and change a thing. Truly, the journey goes on.

CONTENTS

DARKEST OF DAYS

IN THE DARKEST days of 2016, I recall times when I wasn't sure if I would be able to carry on. Thoughts of all the things in my life that were once important were simply gone. At times, I was in a place where I felt like there was nothing left to do; nothing left to live for. I had no reason left to carry on. More than once while driving down the highway, I considered veering into the next lane to meet the semi that was coming towards me head-on.

Those overwhelming thoughts started crossing my mind with ever-greater intensity. A head-on crash with a semi would end it all. I would not have to face the daily dread. I would close my eyes and imagine the semi crashing through the front of my Impala, ramming the engine right through me. Squashing me completely. Tears would roll down my face as I contemplated what the end would look like for me in great detail. With a full tank of gas and traveling at 160 km per hour, I was sure it would be quick and painless.

Part of me gave thought to the fact that I would then get to cross over to the other side and see the loved ones that had gone before me.

My two kids, Sage and Hudson, were what kept me in check.

Thinking of them always brought me back to my senses in mind and spirit. I could not possibly bring myself to go through with ending my own life and leave my kids without a dad! That just was not going to happen. It certainly scared the shit out of me when I had such intense, negative thoughts of self-harm.

I had given lots of thought to how those I left behind would cope without me. I knew there was plenty of life insurance to go around to make sure that my family's needs would all be met, and the rest just wouldn't matter. Oh, how hard those days were!

There were days I didn't eat and nights I didn't sleep. Hours, days, and weeks when I didn't care much to be alive. I found some solace in a few things, one of which was music. I came across a few songs that really struck a nerve with me and hit home with some of the things I was feeling and going through. I was consistently playing songs about heaven or loss or tragedy on my phone. Dancing in the sky was playing daily for quite some time.

I had lost a very good friend of mine in 2005 when he was killed in an underground mining accident at the mine that he and I worked at. In 2006, my dad passed away from a heart attack just shy of 57 years old. In 2010, a friend of mine committed suicide. None of these three events came close to preparing me for losing four of my family members at the same time. The devastation was unbearable.

I was simply at a loss, with no direction as to how to move forward or carry on. Since I was not sleeping during the night, I found myself scrolling through social media on my phone. I ended up coming into contact with others that were going through similar things in their lives and were also up at all hours.

Those 3 am conversations in the middle of the night were what saved me. Rather than shutting down and closing off my feelings, I instead decided that I would start to talk about it. I was pleasantly surprised to learn that the more I shared how I was feeling, both negative and positive, the more I started to understand that it was helping me.

So, I continued to do more.

THE CALL NO ONE EVER WANTS TO RECEIVE

JANUARY 3RD, 2016 was most certainly the worst day of my life. During the wee hours of the morning, my phone rang, waking me up from a deep sleep. The voice on the other end was shaky. It was a local police officer who I had known for a couple of years. He was very to the point, asking where I was and if he could come see me. I instantly knew something was terribly wrong. I was breathing as though my lungs had a two-ton truck squishing them. Oh God, what is he going to say next? I wondered. I was shaking and losing my patience.

I was clear about what I wanted. "What is it, Dave? Please tell me. I can handle it!" I could feel the lump in his throat through the phone. I could just feel that he was shaken to his core. Briefly, I considered my kids, my mom…what could it be? The next few words would change my life forever.

"There has been an accident involving Chanda and Jordan," Dave said. "They were killed instantly."

The silence that likely lingered for only a second seemed days long.

I swallowed the massive lump in my throat. The struggle to form my words was something I had never experienced before. "Dave, how are the kids?" I managed. "Are they ok? Were they in the car too? Dave, tell me…tell me they were somewhere else?"

"They are in critical condition," he replied carefully. "And it doesn't look good."

I fell to my knees on the floor, my sweaty palm barely managing to grasp the cellphone that had delivered the harsh news. It couldn't possibly be true! My mind was blank and numb. I was losing all sense of feeling in my fingers.

"Chad! I am sending an officer over," Dave continued decisively. "Where are you? We can come get you."

He then asked me how we should proceed in getting my mom to the hospital. I was in complete shock, reeling from his devastating words. Hell, I wasn't even sure if I was breathing.

At that point, I realized I was skin to carpet and needed to get dressed. I had to go!

"Dave! Where are they?" I asked.

"They are at Royal University Hospital," he answered.

I spoke quietly, my voice shaking, "I am on my way. I'll make some calls to see how to get mom to the city, and fast."

Oh, God! How would she react? How would Mom take the news that her youngest daughter was gone? How would she carry on? And why was I not there? It was so selfish of me to not even be in a position to get Mom to the hospital. She was going to be a mess! Was there any way the information was wrong? How could this be happening?! It couldn't be, could it? My inner dialogue was in overdrive.

I called a good friend of mine in a panic.

"Mike! Mike, there has been a terrible accident! Chanda and Jordan are dead!" Oh fuck, did those words just come out of my mouth? Without hesitation, Mike agreed to pick up my mom to get her to the hospital. My phone was slippery in my sweaty hand. The rocks in my throat were still there. Choking them down, I ended the call. "Mike, I gotta go! Will call you back right away. Dave is calling me again!"

I took Dave's call. "He…he…he…hell…oooooo," I said in a whisper, my voice trembling. My throat was dry, making it incredibly hard to speak. Dave's response was just as ghostly quiet. "Chad, we are at your mom's house, and her neighbor Doug is here. He is going to get her to the hospital just as soon as he can."

I had known Doug for nearly 20 years, and it gave me some relief to know that Mom had a loving and caring member of our family to help her in this time of utter devastation. He and his family had moved in across the street from us when I was in high school, and we had instantly become like family. Knowing he was there allowed me to breathe again. I knew Mom was in good hands.

Dave assured me that all was well there.

"How is Mom…doing? Is she taking it ok?" I asked.

Dave responded with empathy; kind and considerate in his choice of words. I don't remember exactly what he said, but I do know he calmed my nerves enough for me to allow myself to figure out the next move.

After talking to Dave, I had to call Mike back, knowing full well he was likely in his cold, frozen car waiting for my next instructions. I can only imagine what he was thinking. We had just spent Christmas with them! Mike was part of our family, so I knew he would be devastated too.

"Mike!" I said, my voice still pained and quiet. "Mom has a ride. I'm sorry I woke you up. I don't know what is happening. I don't know what to do. I just called you first because I thought that seemed right. But she has a ride, so we are good. I will keep you posted." That's what I said, as best I can remember. The shock I was experiencing didn't allow clarity, nor did it allow me to remember exactly what I said or the exact timeline of those hours.

I drove across Saskatoon in my Impala. My mind was calm, but my hands were still sweaty, and the rocks were still in my throat. I stuck to the speed limit and was conscious of my driving, perhaps more than ever. I moved across the city effortlessly in what felt like no time at all. Or was it? All the while I was wondering about Kamryn and Miguire.

Were they going to be ok? Had they been strapped in their car seats properly? Of course they had! Jordan and Chanda were both meticulous when it came to their children and safety. A memory flashed through my mind of the last time I had buckled Miguire in his car seat just a few weeks prior, knowing Chanda and Jordan would have done his belts up the same way I had.

It was cold. I remember that for sure. I had my jacket and gloves on because I hadn't allowed the car to warm up. I just turned the key and went. My adrenaline was definitely pumping—I didn't feel the cold, not even a little. The lights were green most of the way, and I only stopped once or twice.

It wasn't until I arrived at the hospital that I recall shedding tears. Up until then, I had been all factual and down to business. All of this had happened in perhaps 15 minutes. I was thankful I was in the city instead of at home at that moment. Perhaps being there an hour sooner would allow me to help in some way. I always helped Miguire and Kamryn in any way I could, so how would this be any different? Surely there was a way to make them better. Hold Miguire's hand maybe. Or whisper something funny in Kamryn's ear. Bring back her smile somehow.

Oh wait, what if they were gone too? I wondered. What if they were d…d…? No, I couldn't even think that word in my mind. Chanda and Jordan were dead. That I had heard so fucking clearly. Mac and Richard (Kamryn's nickname) couldn't be dead too. I couldn't think about it. I just kept wishing I could buckle him in again. Please let me buckle little man in again.

The parking lot at the hospital was mostly empty, and I was able to find a spot easily. Oh God, why was I there? This wasn't real. I wanted to wake up from this bad dream. I couldn't go in. I had to go in. I was so lost and confused. Yet my tears were few. What is actually happening right now? I wondered in a daze.

Into the hospital I went. The ambulances parked outside were switched off. I considered whether the kids had arrived in one of them. It didn't matter. Through the corridor I went, down the hall. I had no idea where to go. I must have asked. Everything was a confusing blur as I was directed up to the fourth floor—ICU.

I don't know if there has ever been a longer elevator ride. The building seemed a thousand floors high, although I knew it wasn't. My son had been on that very floor eight years prior. My stomach was in knots; my thoughts going down a twisted, evil path of nastiness.

ICU required a phone call at the doors to enter the ward, and someone met me at the door once it opened. I don't recall who it was. All I remember was entering the room where they had Miguire. Jordan's mom and dad were there, holding him. He wasn't moving. I was confused.

"How is he doing?" I asked. "What's wrong with him?"

There was an apparatus over his face. I was unsure what it was or why they were using it. It appeared they were pumping it by hand to fill his lungs with air. Why are they doing that? I wondered. I found it weird that he wasn't hooked up to any machines. No doctors were working on him. Was he gone already? Had I missed seeing him? Or had he gone before he arrived? The thoughts and questions rushed through my muddled mind.

Jordan's mom was holding him. We all just stood there looking at him. His lifeless face. He was wrapped in white hospital blankets or towels—I can't remember or don't know which. My little man who had my heart completely wasn't saying uncle. Wasn't moving. No life. No smiles. No nothing.

At some point not long after arriving, I was told they couldn't save him. He too was gone. Once I took that in, once I somehow comprehended it, I was holding him. Was it minutes or half an hour? I haven't a clue. I was holding my favorite human in the world. Clenching him. No, gently squeezing. Why oh why was this happening? He was cold. He wasn't supposed to be cold. Why wouldn't he move?

It is such a strange feeling, being present fully with another body when they are gone. Just gone. Or going…leaving. The breathing apparatus was gone now. We cuddled. We cuddled some more. It was some time before I put my fingertips on his cheeks. So cold. So bitterly cold! I sat in that chair just holding my favorite little man for what felt like hours. Maybe I would wake up and this would all have been a cruel dream.

After some time, he started turning blue. Getting colder. Losing his color. Lifeless. He had been so full of energy just days before. "Ockee! Pay ockee!! Uncle pay ockeee!"

We just sat in shocked silence. In disbelief. How could this be happening? Can't you take me instead of little man?! Please take me!

Other people started to arrive. Mom and Doug were there. My ex-wife Melanie. Jordan's siblings. My oldest sister Tana and her husband James. Such a blur. So much chaos. Who arrived when, I'm not sure.

Kamryn! What about Kamryn? The mind fog was so prevalent that I am unclear at what point I even asked about Kamryn. I learned that she was the only one of the four that they had any sort of hope in saving. She had suffered a tremendous blow to the head. My heart was crushed at the first sight of her lying in a bed in a room across the hall from Miguire's room.

The gash that she had over her face and into her hairline was enough to make us all gasp for air. The doctors and nurses told us that she was likely brain-damaged or possibly brain-dead. A test was scheduled to determine the severity of her head injuries. We waited somberly for what seemed like an eternity. How could this possibly be? What if she was brain-damaged or brain-dead? What would this all mean?

As we waited, we took turns holding Miguire in Kamryn's room. Moments turned to minutes, which lead into hours. We all said our goodbyes in our own ways. Nothing prepares you for holding a two-year-old and saying your last goodbye. The feeling of an empty heart. The desperate desire to change places. Please just take a breath little buddy! Please, I beg of you to come back! You can't go. How could this happen? Even though he had turned cold hours ago and was very blue, I still thought those things over and over.

Watching the doctors perform the test to see if Kamryn was brain-dead was quite possibly one of the calmest and most spiritual experiences I have ever had in my entire life. They disconnected her ventilator to see if she could breathe on her own. She had all kinds of monitors, machines, and tubes hooked up to her.

I believe there were two family members in the room at this point. The others couldn't bear to see what was going to happen to her body; to the most precious little girl on the planet. I held her little hand. She seemed so warm and cozy under the heated blanket, which was helping keep her organs alive by regulating her temperature.

I thought that perhaps my holding her hand and having someone she knew in the room would make it less painful or perhaps bring her some peace. The team of doctors and nurses disconnected and shut off all the machines. There was a minute or so of almost dead silence. Kamryn's body lay lifeless. Her fingers were not moving against mine. Not even a twitch.

The doctors started and reconnected all the machines again. I could see Kamryn's chest inflating with air again. The color returned to her skin. I knew—we all knew—she was gone. She was to go with the rest of her family. We all thought of what would happen if she survived and had major challenges. Would it be best for her to be with the other three members of her family? Yes, yes of course she should be with them, together as a family unit. Whole and complete. Four angels as one.

Our insides were ripped from us yet again. The news wasn't good. Kamryn was clinically brain-dead, which meant without the machines keeping her alive, there was no way for her to come back. There was no way for us to hear her amazing laugh and see her infectious smile ever again. The devastation was so real! Our hearts were all broken. We were all broken. Even the nurses and doctors were all broken.

It was then said that Kamryn would need to have the same test performed yet again to ensure that the same results were obtained. Oh God, how could I do this again? But I had to. I needed to. By this time, I was breathing slowly. Short breaths, calm and peaceful. It was like the spirits and souls of my two favorite little ones were with me. As though the blood flowing through my veins had gained their blood. I knew I was to hold her hand again. One more test. One more time that her body would likely not move in any way. Her lungs wouldn't move. No gasp for air. A state of nothingness.

Again, the same result. Essentially, she was pronounced dead. What would happen now? What was next? There was some discussion around whether or not we would consider organ donation. It honestly took us just a few minutes to unanimously decide. Yes, we would absolutely donate her organs. Kamryn was one of the most spirited children I had ever met. She reminded me so much of my oldest son. Full of so much energy and so much zest for life. A natural curiosity for all things. We knew her little body needed to be part of someone else's. That energy and spunk would surely be a life force for someone else. We all knew it was the right thing to do. Chanda would have absolutely wanted that, and so would Jordan.

At some point that day, I needed to make some phone calls. I needed to tell some people what had happened. Holy shit, where to start?! I picked up the phone and called my closest cousins, aunts, and uncles. Just as I had received the call from officer Dave perhaps 12 hours earlier, I was now the one delivering the same news. Only I was delivering the news that they were all gone. There were no maybes or possibilities that one of them might have a chance. There was no talk of one of them in critical condition.

"Hello Jodi, this is Chad…" I said, my voice shaky, quiet, and broken. "I have some very bad news." Jodi responded in the same way as most others I called.

"Chad, what is wrong, what happened?"

The tears rolled down my face. "It's not good, cousin. There was a terrible car accident, and Chanda and Jordan and the kids are all gone!" Everyone was devastated.

That day I broke so many hearts. My own heart broke more and more with each call I had to make. So many family members and friends. I quickly realized that I couldn't handle too many, so I planned my calls. I called one cousin, uncle, or aunt in each family and asked them to tell their families. I asked them to start spreading the word. I don't know if hearing the news myself had been harder than calling family to tell them the same. It was so hard to do, and so hard on my heart and soul. It crushed me. It crushed us all.

I vividly remember the painful screams and squeals I heard on the other end of the line. The bursting into tears. The unfathomable thoughts of their hearts feeling what I was feeling. Their minds searching for some understanding when there wasn't any. Over and over I heard, "Oh my God Chad, that can't be true!" Some of the people I called were silent for some time. The shock prevented any words from coming out.

At one-point police officers came to explain to us what had happened. The gentleman that started talking to us when we were all gathered in the family room on the ICU ward was sharp with his words, at least initially. He told us what he had come upon. He had been first on scene. His voice cracked as he explained that he and his partner were literally right there when it happened.

He spoke of what he saw, and my mind remained stuck on just a small portion of his words.

"After assessing things with all the passengers, I was holding Miguire's hand," he said. I had the sense and understanding from the officer's words that he thought Miguire's was the only life that could perhaps have been saved. He thought that there was some inkling or twinkle of existence left. Or maybe it was that he felt he needed to hold his hand as he was passing away into nothingness. My little man was not alone, I thought. This very wonderful soul had offered his hand to Miguire in his last moments.

I do not recall much else of what the officer shared with us that day. He did say that the driver had been intoxicated and that she was searching frantically for her phone when she got out of her smashed jeep. Her words had made very little sense, in fact, she thought she was the one who had been hit.

My mind was racing. Was there a reason for all this? What was happening? Did this just happen? I was having a very hard time wrapping my mind around the events that had transpired.

That first day in the ICU we learned that all four of our favorite people were gone. Just wiped off the physical planet as we knew it. Doctors, nurses, monitors, and machines. How could we carry on? What was to happen next?

At one point, some of us left the hospital to try to get some rest. I recall I slept some, however I don't believe it was much. The next day we were to head back to the hospital to arrange Kamryn's organ donation process. But I found myself unable to leave the home I was staying in. I kept throwing up, and I couldn't leave the washroom. My mind was full of a thousand thoughts and emotions; I was unable to process them at all. My body had plans of its own, purging all that it could. Releasing all its contents.

Everyone else was at the hospital for the day. We were all incredibly lucky to know that Kamryn would make such a huge difference in the world, even through such tragic circumstances. Her heart went to Stollery Hospital in Edmonton, where someone was very fortunate to have her heart transplanted to them.

To this day, I think of Kamryn's heart often. How is the recipient doing? Where are they from? Was he able to recover fully as a little guy just doing normal little boy things? The thought makes me smile. Makes me wonder. Oh, I hope he is vibrant and healthy like Kamryn was. I really believe he must be.

Her lungs were too damaged to be transplanted, but most of her other organs were all used. Some went to Ontario, where one recipient received multiple organs from Kamryn. I often wonder how those people are doing with the wonderful gifts they received from Kamryn.

From others' accounts of the day I missed, I learned that it was a very somber day. Knowing that Kamryn was going down the hall to the OR where her organs would be harvested for a higher purpose, I truly believe we all held on to the fact that a true angel was spreading her wings, literally breathing life into other people.

A MOTHER'S PAIN

ON DAY THREE, they brought Chanda and Jordan's bodies to the bottom floor in the hospital for us to view. I had no idea where they were during the first 48 hours or perhaps more, as we were focused on the littles. The bodies were transported in from across the city to allow us to say goodbye, no, maybe to say see you again or confirm that it was all real. Our thoughts were scattered; our hearts all broken in pieces.

The extreme anguish on Mom's face was one of the toughest things I have had to see in my life. Watching her lay eyes on her youngest daughter's lifeless body, I really don't know how our knees were holding us up. How it was even possible to comprehend or carry on through the day. We had no consideration for food nor sleep. We just needed to be present because that is all there was.

We walked into the room and saw both bodies stretched out on gurneys, cold and lifeless. Colorless. The room was filled with this intense, draining energy of sadness and unfathomable sorrow. My family went in as a unit, as did Jordan's. To grieve. To hold. To be. Is there anything else to do? Be? We were completely overcome with emotion, from head to toe. Chanda's body was strewn in an awkward way with her arm up and bent unnaturally. Someone explained to us that her arm was severely broken. They had placed it in that way so as to not really disturb it.

Jordan's body appeared like he was just sleeping. We all knew otherwise, as his head showed severe trauma. His skull was misshapen. I felt instant pains in my head as I saw my brother-in-law in a state of ruin. It was hard not to see flashes of a car going 130 km an hour and slamming into his head. He had taken the hit directly, as the car would have plowed straight into the driver's side door.

Officer Matt had told us a few days earlier that Jordan was driving the car, Chanda was in the passenger seat, Miguire directly behind his daddy, and Kamryn behind her mommy. I struggled to keep the thoughts from my head of the front bumper plummeting into Jordan's skull at more than full speed, imagining what happened to the car seats that the two little angels were in upon impact.

In that small room we distraughtly honored Chanda and Jordan for who they were. Sad for who they might have been. Two people full of life and greatness gone—Just gone. I don't recall if everyone touched them or what was said. My mind doesn't really know what took place. Were we in there for moments, minutes, or hours? I just don't know.

I placed my hands on my little sister's face. I wanted to feel. I wanted to hold. I knew it would be cold, as I had done the same a decade ago when my dad died and a few other friends as well. I knew about the energy transfer that happens. Chanda was my closest friend, my best friend, the one I shared my entire life with. She was so cold; just so cold. Her smile was gone.

I was overcome by an overwhelming sense of loss. No more daily calls to chat about life and kids. No more get-togethers filled with laughter. No more wisdom from my confidant who knew my entire life and all we shared. Chanda was most definitely the one person on the planet that understood me completely and was aware of all my celebrations and shortcomings in every sense. Her extremely kind and caring heart and always quick life advice were to be no longer. I felt as though a huge part of me was lying lifeless on that cold table.

It was no different with Jordan. I couldn't help but think of the amazing things he had done and would have done as I gently touched his cheeks, held his hand, and spoke soft words to him. Without thinking, my hands slowly felt into his hairline. I was curious if I would be able feel his misshapen skull. As if to repair it. To make it better.

To my recollection, I don't believe there was much talk between us. The words just weren't there. We thought and felt as one. We were with them. It was so unbelievably hard to stand in that moment. Were they still in the conceivable world somehow, or in some magical place of peace?

Four faces had graced the forever-changed surface of my hands in just a few days. Those days seemed like an eternity; time was not moving. I remember having a sense of peace come over me after seeing their lifeless corpses and speaking our last few words. Softly spoken; to be remembered forever.

The most difficult thoughts that weighed heavy on my heart was that I wouldn't be able to call my sister whenever I wanted, nor would I ever be able to hold Miguire's tiny little hands again; his little fingers wrapped around one of mine.

In the days that followed, we planned and executed the most amazing TRIBUTE OF LOVE! Thanks to Tana for coining the phrase that best describes how I think of them. With 1200 people from all over the country attending, it was epic. We laughed and we cried. We visited with people near and far. We remembered and cherished. Held and steadied. We did what we needed to do.

All four bodies were cremated and laid to rest in an urn specially picked out for four wonderful beings. They have a special place in the cemetery near the outside edge where, almost every time I am there, I see rabbits and crows. As Miguire would have liked, there are train tracks not too far away. I marvel at the trains passing by on occasion when I am there.

The following months were filled with more anguish and

heart-clenching times. What was to happen to their stuff? We had to take care of the house, the car, and the contents of the house right from groceries to toys to clothes.

Walking into their house was unsettling. It was hard to see their everyday things still strewn about. Dirty dishes in the sink, a fridge stocked full of groceries from Costco that Chanda had bought just the day before the accident. Dirty laundry downstairs and clean laundry set aside but not put away yet. Where to start?

We took the things we held close to our hearts first, such as the last Christmas gifts we had given them. I was quick to spot the mini sticks I had given Miguire less than a week before they had gone, as well as the Barbie doll I had given Kamryn. To this day, I still have them in my room.

One of the worst parts I believe was that we were unsure as to whether or not there was a will or insurance policies and where they might be. Between the time we were in the hospital and the funeral, we were at the house searching through filing cabinets and drawers in the hope of finding clues to wills and/or insurance. We discovered that they did not have wills. The insurance policies we found were looked after when we had the chance.

We found pictures and more pictures everywhere! Thank goodness for all the amazing photography that Jordan had done, with the kids especially. There were thousands of pictures, and we were all super grateful for them. Hard copies, pics on cameras, pics on computers; pics everywhere.

Disposing of all their belongings seemed like a formality. With the exception of the few cherished items we had taken, all the other belongings were split up amongst Jordan's family and mine. Food from the freezer and fridge found a different home, the toys were donated to a local charity, the furniture was either taken by a family member or sold, clothes were mostly donated, with a few items finding their way into some of our closets, and the yard stuff was handled in much the same way.

As we went through the process of disposal, I learned just how attached some of us were to certain items. It was a way of not letting go yet. It seemed as though having that one item that reminded you of them would somehow lessen the hurt and pain. I found myself often holding the mini sticks that Miguire had used at Christmas. I would clench them as if I could feel his little fingers holding them. It wasn't until the summer of 2018 that I was able to actually give away some of them. The first one I put in the ground with the urn when we buried them. I am left with two, and they sit on my dresser at home.

They mean something different to me now. It's not that they are my last hope to see them again like it may have been early on. Now they are more a reminder of the amazing few days I had with Miguire putting his very first hockey stick into his hands. Did he ever love it, and so did I! It filled my heart with joy to see him so very happy to play hockey. When I occasionally look at the mini stick on my dresser, it makes me smile as I take myself back to such a joyous time with such a wonderful human being.

Even the Barbie doll I have on my dresser makes me smile. Although I wasn't there when Kamryn was playing with her new Barbie, it was already missing an arm within a week. She played hard and she had fun. Her imagination and tenacity reminded me of my oldest son. She played so hard that destruction was inevitable. It sure makes me smile even as I write this. Mrs. Barbie with the purple hair and missing arm fills my heart with great thoughts and memories.

Next came the task of selling the house. Yes, it was merely a task, as none of us wanted anything to do with that house any longer. It served no purpose nor had any value to any of us in any way. We brought in a realtor and took his advice on how to list it in the best way possible. The walls needed to be washed and painted to give us the best showing. Some of us did not see the point in painting. However, as a group, the final decision was to put the best show home on the market we could so that we had the best chances of selling it as soon as possible. Once the contents were gone, we all just wanted the house sold as quickly as possible. We could not bear to go there any more than we had to; it was too painful.

To the best of my recollection, there were very few house showings and we had a solid offer soon enough. In May of the same year, the house was sold for a fair dollar that we were happy to get.

We sent many letters and made many calls to cancel all the things they were involved in. Power, water, energy, phones, memberships, and the like. Jordan's mom in particular put in many exhausting hours to look after all these tedious things. I for one was incredibly grateful to her for taking care of all these things.

JUSTICE AND LEGALITIES

THERE IS NO doubt in my mind that before the tragic car crash, I was fairly naive when it came to the legal system and court proceedings. Other than what I had seen on television, my knowledge of the law and penalties for crimes was virtually non-existent. Even when I would hear about some sentencing that was handed down on the news, I chose not to put much thought into it. I wasn't very worldly on that front and therefore had a tremendous amount of learning to do when we were forced into a court case we never wanted anything to do with.

Generally speaking, I am an understanding person for the most part and always willing to hear and consider both sides of the story. That said, nothing could have possibly prepared me to be understanding of the woman who had killed my family in a most heinous way.

I heard of other similar cases where the convicted was sentenced to just a few months. Others were behind bars for many years. It was a lot to take in, and it was hard to think that she might only be locked up for a few short years. Of course, I went through many stages—anger, grief, sadness, devastation, and complete inner turmoil. However, I needed to learn and form my own opinions.

From January to May it seemed we were forever dealing with household items and wrapping up their daily affairs. Once that seemed like it was behind us, it was time for the court case. July 27th, 2016 was the date they had set for Catherine McKay to learn her fate.

We had a few meetings with lawyers and the crown prosecutor to discuss sentencing and how the court case would go. The family discussed what we wanted to happen and how the prosecutor was proceeding. We agreed that it was very important to go for the maximum penalty in Canada. To date, there were very few cases where four lives were taken at once, and the crown prosecutor was going to fight for the highest possible penalty.

Of course, with anger and other emotions bubbling from us, we were talking about a 15 or 20 year sentence. The emotions in those meetings were very intense, more so for some than for others. It was amazing to see the vast differences in emotions and feelings between the half dozen or more of us attending those meetings. The crown prosecutor assured us that he was really going to put his best case forward in the hope of securing the toughest penalty our country had ever seen for such a case.

We were all encouraged to write victim impact statements. These statements are designed to be read aloud in court with the defendant present to hear how the victims are affected by what they had done. The process of writing my impact statement was definitely the hardest thing I have ever done. It was incredibly difficult to put into words what our lost loved ones meant to us and how their death hurt us to the core. With their deaths so fresh in our minds, writing about it was emotionally charged, to say the least. The tears flowed easily when thinking about it and putting it all onto paper.

I recall writing my statement and wondering how in the hell I was possibly going to be able to speak those words out loud in court with Catherine McKay just steps away from me. How would I be able to convey my forever-broken heart to her so she would understand how I felt? How we all felt. She would have to FEEL it to get it.

The full wheel of emotions and thoughts were at the forefront of my mind while thinking about and writing my victim impact statement.

Anger and rage, at first towards Catherine McKay, and then towards the cruel world we live in with all the unjust things it brings us in life. It is just so unfair how four people can just be taken from us in an instant.

I began writing my statement a dozen times and tossed all of them in the garbage. Tears flowed down my face and I felt sad and empty. I could not comprehend how I could possibly put into words how this crime was affecting me in every way possible. I was hard on myself in that I thought the statement had to be perfect. I also remember thinking that somehow my words needed to cut deep into Catherine's heart. I needed to convey just how much her actions had hurt us all so, so badly.

I knew it would be an excruciating and painful day when we were to read our statements in court. So many broken hearts pouring out all the hurt and pain. I could not help but have a mental image of us all crying and reading our statements while I was struggling to put my thoughts onto paper. Finally, after a few days, I was able to land my thoughts on talking only towards the judge. If I stared at him as though there were no other people in the room, perhaps I could get through it. That was when the words started to come a little easier, although I was still filled with tears, endless anger, and pain.

Leading up to the court date I thought about seeing her eyes. I wanted to look directly into Catherine McKay's eyes, as if to throw daggers from my soul into hers. I wanted to scar her deeply, as she had done to me. I was so full of anger and rage. I wanted revenge! There had to be a repayment of some sort.

I have never been as nervous in my entire life as I was the morning of the court date. We planned to all arrive at the same time to show our solidarity as two families grieving and suffering. Was it also to show strength when none of us felt strong at all? I felt that together, we were supporting each other as best we could, holding one another up at a time when our minds and bodies were the weakest they had ever been. We entered the courthouse as a group, not knowing what was coming at all.

For the first time since this had all started, we finally had a chance to see Catherine McKay in person. She was to be in court to learn her fate as a result of her actions. Most of us wanted to see how she would react. Was she going to show emotion? Would she have anything to say? So many questions and thoughts raced through my mind.

She read her statement in a quiet voice. I have a hard time recalling what she said. I do remember her words about living the rest of her life being an advocate against drinking and driving to prevent this from happening to others. Those words sat top of mind for me in a way I would not understand until I started the process of writing this book.

I replayed those words in my mind over and over again, pondering them with skepticism. Was she for real? Did she actually truly mean what she said? Or were her words a fabricated statement coerced by her legal team? I wondered about this hundreds of times. I even considered how I would have reacted if I were in her shoes.

Hearings those words for the first time did bring me a small sense of relief in that she genuinely seemed sorry for her actions. I also believed that she was capable of making a difference in the future to prevent others from making the same mistake. As her words were on repeat in my mind for weeks and months afterwards, they took on more and more meaning for me.

That day in court, we all read our victim impact statements, overcome with emotion like never before. I had a very difficult time reading my statement, so much so that I wasn't even sure if anyone understood a single word. Others had as much of a hard time as I did. Kamryn's kindergarten teacher also read a statement, as did the police officer who had been first on scene.

I specifically remember scanning the room to see who was there. About 40 people filled the seats. I noticed two people who looked to me like they might have been Catherine's children. They sure looked a lot like her. For a minute I sat with that. I wondered how they were doing. Were they there because they supported their mom? Or were they there to learn what the court's sentence would be? Were they able to go see her in prison or talk to her on the phone? Most of these thoughts crossed my mind that day and some came not too many days after.

That day we heard that the crown prosecutor and Catherine's lawyer had come to an agreement on the sentencing, and the judge was on board with it. She was to serve 10 years in prison less time served on four counts of impaired driving causing death. July 27th, 2016 was perhaps the darkest day of my life. I was so very broken and empty, with nothing left. How could we carry on from there?

The next few months were a complete blur. I suppose I was running my businesses and hanging out with my kids when I could. I really don't have any recollection of most of those days, weeks, and months. My short-term memory was all but gone during that time. I was relying heavily on my kids and their momma for direction most days and weeks. I had a conversation with Angela more than once to ask her to please remind me of the things that were happening with our kids; when and where they had to be. Otherwise I would just forget. Some days I would forget to pick them up from school or that there was supposed to be hockey or band. Simple things became hard.

Sometime in September of that year, Catherine was transferred from prison to a healing lodge in southern Saskatchewan, where she remained until April 2020. The media and general public made a huge story of it, and people were in a big panic about it all. News outlets ran the story in every way possible, and my phone was going off yet again.

In the first few conversations I had with people about this, I just listened to their opinions and chose to stay calm. I got sick of it all, and fast. I couldn't handle it any longer. I finally started to speak up before people could share their thoughts with me. I was blunt—I had to be. I told them all that they could keep their opinions to themselves. Where Catherine served her sentence and for how long had zero impact on me by that point. It wouldn't change the hurt or pain I was going through in any way, nor would it bring back my family.

I found myself responding to posts online on Facebook about the court case and about her sentencing and where she was. Some of those conversations became heated. It seemed like I was one of very few people who were coming from a place that wasn't filled with anger and rage. For a few months, I took part in many of these conversations, both in person and on social media. It became too much, so I stopped.

In the fall of 2016 there was a bit of a lull. After we dissolved all the house's contents, sold the house, and went through the court case and sentencing, it seemed as though that was that. Then it became apparent and real that it was time to deal with my thoughts and my feelings. How could I possibly carry on? How could I possibly pick up the pieces and put them back together?

Sleep became elusive. I was up at all hours of the night, up early in the morning, sleepy all day, and always tired. It seemed as though I started living a double life. I started reaching out to people to talk about my experiences and how I was feeling. That led me into a lot of different conversations about real-life situations, events, tragedies, loss, suicide, drinking, alcohol, drugs—so many different things. I found myself talking to people over messenger, text, or phone calls at night.

It was as though we were helping each other through difficult things in our life. I became very aware of just how many people in this world are hurting, and in so many different ways.

At some point in November of that year, I started noticing that my short term memory and a little bit of clarity was returning to my mind. This allowed me to adopt a different mindset. I was starting to understand how I was feeling and how I was dealing with things on a deeper level. I started noticing that I wasn't forgetting as many things anymore and I was starting to become more present with my kids. It seemed as though the weight on my shoulders had started to lessen.

Once I was at a point where I better understood how I was moving through the process of grief and loss, I began thinking about the things I had checked out of for most of the year. Businesses that were operating at far less than they should have been, my life that was basically put on hold, and my kids that really didn't have a father for that year.

So where would I go from here? How could I repair my heart and the damage that was inside me? Who was I now? It felt like there was a big void in my life and a hole in my heart. I became overwhelmed with feelings and thoughts of sinking; being on a ship that was going down. I was unsure how to move forward and carry on.

(1) Chad McEwan Statement

Victim Impact Statement

On Jan 03 2016 my sister, brother in law, niece and nephew were killed in a car accident. I am writing this statement today in an attempt to convey just how this tragic event has affected me. There really is no possible way to put into words how I am effected or how much it has changed my life.

Since Jan 03 I have had a great deal of difficulty concentrating and my memory is terrible. From Jan - March I had to ask my kids everything such as what days they have what activities and what times. I forgot what day it is, forget to pick them up from dance or hockey, forget to buy the things they need for school lunches. I am self employed and run four businesses and it has been so hard to keep things running at their very least. I find myself doing things now in June that I typically do in Jan or Feb. Just so far behind. What used to take me a few hours now takes me a day or two.

Emotionally, I find that most days I am on the edge of tears. Any little thing could set me off. All the things that Kamryn and Maguire would have been doing now just play on my mind each and every day. Watching my son play hockey makes me think of Miguire and how he liked to watch the Zamboni go around the ice or how I was just getting started on teaching him about hockey. Christmas time I bought him mini sticks and he loved playing hockey. Or when my youngest son has dance Kamryn loved watching dance and as she got older was wanting to try dancing. Other parents ~~look~~ look at me during my sons dance and wonder why i'm crying, its because I see Kamryn on stage dancing but she never had the chance. Two bright vibrant beautiful children taken from this world before they had a chance to try these things they wanted to try. My new normal is a day filled with sorrow and sadness, a day wishing to have all four back in my ~~life~~ life. ~~Chad~~ Chanda was my go to person on a daily ~~basis~~ basis. She was my confidant, my one non judgemental person I could share anything and everything with. She is gone now and there is a huge gap in my life and in each day. Jordan too, his sense of humor his passion for the little things in life. Gone too.

3) [illegible] Statement

There are so many changes in my life. Besides being forgetful and having poor concentration I dont eat much, sleep isn't nearly as good as it once was. I am short with my kids, and seem to be pre occupied with thought rather than spending time with my kids. This simply is not fair to my two boys or to myself.

Economically, I would say has been unmeasurable. The businesses I run are perhaps running at 20-30% of what they normally would be. Bills unpaid, books not done yet, customers not happy etc. all because I am so far behind and because I cannot concentrate to do things how they should be done. I have told all my employees and friends that they need to help me out and be patient with me. Everyday is a struggle. The financial loss is huge, perhaps $100,000 to date just because I am simply not who I used to be. I loved those four so much and they are on my mind always.

The fact is, I dont eat, sleep or carry on a daily routine like I used to. Always so tired and so emotional. My mind shuts down, my body shuts down. Some days I do very little because I dont care or I just cant do it. That really sucks because I used to have dreams of running many more businesses and being very successful but now i'm not so sure. No one can bring them back and maybe someday I will improve with my mind and body but I don't Know at this point.

There is more too. I have to worry about my oldest sister and my mom. Will they be OK or will they fall apart from the stresses that come along with this tragedy. My two boys also. Since Jan 03 their attitudes, emotions and behaviours have been altered drastically. At 11 and 13 it seems they are lashing out at school, grades dropping, fights with friends etc. It's just so much piling up and lots to deal with. And how do I discipline my kids for these things when there is no doubt the cause is from losing their Uncle, Aunt and two little cousins. Again so not fair at all. Everyday its a challenge to make sure my boys, mom, and sister are doing OK. My ex wife Melanie is also struggling a great deal and that to has affected me a lot. So many of us that have got to find a new normal, one in which is missing four very close family members. Love you always and forever Chanda, Jordan, Kamryn, and Miguire!!!

THE QUIET AND RESILIENT STRENGTH

AS A MAN, I tend to do my best to fix things, but after the painful loss of a huge part of our family, I was having a hard time "fixing" anything, particularly with my family members. There was no way to help my mom; or that was my perception at least. How could I help someone who was so hurt and full of pain? I could see her brokenness clearly.

The fixer in me was on high alert, wondering just how I could help my mom and sister as well as my sons. Initially I had these thoughts each day. However, as time passed, I realized I couldn't help anyone else until I helped myself. It's a crushing feeling knowing that as a man, son, brother, and father, I was all but useless to anyone for months and months.

I don't know how hard it was for the rest of our family for most of 2016, as I just couldn't deal with anyone else but myself. Most days, the best it got was getting dressed and feeding myself. Over the course of three, four, or five months, I slowly emerged from what I call the grief fog.

Once my thoughts and feelings became somewhat sorted and less volatile, I was able to start lending my hand and heart again. I was able to ask someone else how they were doing without feeling like I was going to cry myself.

Even if I didn't quite ask the questions, I was at least able to start noticing how others around me were coping; who was really struggling mentally and/or emotionally.

My heart broke many times as I watched my own mother shed tears for many different reasons. Each time it left another little scar inside me somewhere. It was just not fair to see her hurting so deeply.

At times, the anger and rage inside of her seemed like it was ready to boil over. She was quick to snap and was sharp with her tongue at times. And still, I had a hard time landing on any constructive way to help alleviate the hurt and pain for her.

Sometimes it was as simple as offering a listening ear and making a suggestion or two to guide her towards something I thought might help. Other times it was observing and asking others for suggestions.

I will forever be grateful for the local Victim Services representative, Tracy, who checked in with my mom and myself from time to time. She quickly became someone I trusted and leaned on. I cannot say enough of the wonderful, kind, and caring soul that shed tears with me on the other end of the line. Her unwavering care and attention to my family's and my well-being will never be forgotten nor discounted.

At times she was all I had. I could call her anytime during working hours and just spill it all. Just talk. Share my thoughts and feelings. I often asked her for advice about other family members, including my mom. Tracy spent many calls chatting with Mom as well, and I'm sure she helped her as much as she helped me.

Mom had times of incredible frustration. This I know, as did we all. I remember one particular time when she was doing the dishes and Tana (my oldest sister) was home to visit her. Coming up the stairs, Tana heard Mom cursing at the dishes with great anger.

On another occasion, Mom was face-to-face with me and was just short of screaming at me. I was filled with bewilderment, as this just wasn't the quiet and caring Momma I had known my whole life.

Sure that I was also doing some things that were definitely out of sorts for me, I did my best to figure out how to help Mom through those tough days and times. Often I just listened. Other times I helped out by doing what needed to be done around her house or yard.

Looking back on those days, I wonder if sometimes I did those things for her or to make me feel better. Perhaps both at the same time. There really is no describing how such a tragic loss can mess up someone's emotions and feelings, and how they can often pop up in unexpected ways and situations.

I believe it would be fair to say that my mom's grief journey, being far different than mine, was just as hard, if not harder. We all navigated through the grief in our own way and still are. I also know it was and is hard for me as her son to watch her in so much pain. It was awful to feel so completely helpless when all I wanted to do was to make it all go away for her.

I occasionally suggested counseling and having people to talk to, as I had done a lot of both. However, Mom was far less open to the idea. I know she did see one or two people, as she spoke of it not helping or that she didn't like them. I became frustrated with it all more than once.

In the fall of 2018, she attended a three-day program that I know for a fact was a big help to her and to us all. I attended the same course in February of 2018, and Tana in July of the same year. It was called PSI Seminars, and I would suggest that anyone and everyone should absolutely invest three days of their time to learn more about themselves! The program is very good.

After taking the three-day course, there was a change in Mom. She seemed to carry herself a little differently. It was refreshing to see her smile and laugh a little more fully and lightly again. I got the sense that she had worked through some things, and that lifted my spirits too.

My mom is the softest, most gentle human on the planet. A woman of quiet yet abundant strength, with a work ethic that far surpasses most people half her age. It was incredibly hard to see her spirit squashed and shattered. Once a few years had passed and I was seeing that spark of hers ignite again, I felt I was walking with a little more pep in my step myself. I had a sense that things were going to be ok.

After all, we all want nothing more than to have happy and healthy parents. With Dad gone for many years already, it was even tougher to see her going through what she did.

I love her dearly for who she is, unconditionally, always and forever. Never will I be anywhere close to as strong and resilient as she is. One day I hope to be as powerful in my own right, just like she is!

MIERAU FAMILY

FROM THE DEPTHS of the barren, underground Potash mine I surfaced to a bone-chilling -38 Celsius morning above ground, where my more-than-frozen car awaited. Like many mornings, I ventured home with longing thoughts of a different career. The winter of 2013 was a chilly one in Saskatchewan, and I found myself yearning for a career that would fulfill me. I really felt that I wasn't living fully, nor was I living my purpose. In fact, I really hadn't considered what my purpose even was. I was good at running equipment and fixing things. I was a potash miner and I had also just started to dabble in real estate. My wife at the time and I had dreams of being real estate moguls in our own right, with plans to expand and grow in a very big way.

Growing up on a family farm where I learned all I knew from my parents was truly a blessing, although I didn't realize it fully just yet. My father was incredibly good at teaching my brother and I a plethora of skills on the grain farm we ran at the time; right from running equipment to plumbing and electrical. He was forever a giver and a teacher guiding me, my brother, and my two sisters, and he gave us an incredible start in the world.

So often I wondered why my brother and I had to work on the farm for what seemed like most days, missing out on some of the things children could and should be doing. I found myself feeling disappointed that I didn't have the opportunity to play football or hang out after school like the other kids. To me it seemed it was always work and farming, each day. Sure, there were times that I did have the choice and I did get to be a kid. However, at that time, all I saw was the desire to be a kid rather than work on the farm so much.

As a youngster, I played hockey in the winter when farming was slow. So did my brother Tyler and my sister Chanda. In her early years, my oldest sister Tana was into figure skating, and that made our family winters full of exciting times at the rink for practices, games, tournaments, and figure skating events to pass the cold Canadian winters. All four of us were very involved in band, with my oldest sister eventually getting her degree in education specializing in band. Her specialty was the piano, and our house was forever filled with music in one form or another. Tana became a very talented pianist, taking our family to many places in Saskatchewan for her performances at different venues such as music festivals, concerts, and musicals.

Chanda was the youngest of four in our family. She pursued hockey with the boys program in our local town of Watrous until she was 15. At that time, she started playing elsewhere, with women's teams in Saskatchewan taking her career to different levels. She was good enough to keep up with all the boys locally and excelled on her women's teams as well. Her hockey career eventually took her to the university level, where she played for the University of Saskatchewan while she was enrolled in the Kinesiology program. She completed her course and had a great hockey career with the university.

Tyler was the third eldest among my siblings and I. He was always very smart and dismantled many things as a kid to understand how they worked. This eventually led him into mechanical engineering. He took a position in Fort McMurray, Alberta for just over a year while studying engineering. Once he was through his university program, he became a full-time employee with Suncor in Fort McMurray.

Our mom was and is a kind, caring, soft-spoken, mild-mannered woman with unsurpassed strength and knowledge. While Dad, my brother, and I kept the farm in order, Mom and my two sisters would work on keeping the household running as efficiently as possible. I remember Mom bringing meals to the farm many days while we were well into seeding or harvesting. Some of my favorite memories as a child were those days when we would shut down long enough to have a meal that Mom had so lovingly prepared for us. Almost always, those days were also filled with memories of throwing the football around and jumping over swaths. My brother, me, and my dad would often throw a long ball to see if we could run full-out to catch it while simultaneously jumping swaths to get there.

My brother and I marveled at how well Dad could throw the football so many years after being the quarterback in his high school days. I had a knack for tossing the pigskin nearly as far as Dad by the time I was 16. I remember the day I was finally able to do that. If you could imagine two kids and their father throwing a football in a field during harvest, that was us. We did it often; or at least, that is how I remember it.

Once we were all through high school, Dad slowly phased out of farming. He went from approximately 2500 acres with my brother and I helping to just a few hundred himself in a matter of a few short years after my brother and I left the family home. He rented out some of the land while he farmed the rest for a short period of time and eventually sold all but a half section, which he ended up renting to one of our farming neighbors.

Through the years in our early 20s, all us kids got into relationships and started down our own career paths. I was the only one of the four kids that did not obtain a post-secondary degree. I did however attend university for one year with a very unclear direction as to what I wanted to do. I ended up back in my hometown after one year of post-secondary to pursue work as a mechanic, taking apart farm equipment at a local salvage yard.

It was apparent early on that my youngest sister Chanda would be the one who had the ability to keep us all together. She had the most pull in bringing us together under the same roof as a family for holiday times, birthdays, anniversaries, and the like. She was most definitely the sibling I was the closest to. In fact, she was my best friend for many years. She became the one I talked to most often—almost daily for the most part. There was nothing she didn't know about me and my life. She was my confidante; my go-to person for all things, from good to bad and everywhere in-between.

Chanda always had a smile on her face, and she had the kindest and most caring heart on the entire planet. This carried through into her eventual career as a sports therapist helping people rehabilitate from injury and pain. I believe she was more than that, though. Her kind heart allowed her to operate in her job in a way where she would influence everyone around her in such a positive way. Even if it was just a very short interaction, people would walk away in a better mood or feeling better than before they spoke to or saw her. Her smile was infectious and bright, and her eyes were full of life and had much to share. Her demeanor was pleasant and calm. She just had a very special way about her.

The age-old custom of getting a job, getting married, and having kids was true for all four of us to a certain extent. I was the first to have children. My son Sage came into this world in April of 2003 and Hudson a few short years later in April 2005. Another few years later, my brother Tyler had three boys of his own. Chanda and Jordan would have Kamryn and Miguire in 2011 and 2013. Life seemed to be moving along just as it should.

That was until May 2006, when I received news while at work underground that my dad had suddenly passed away at home. As a family, we were shocked and devastated, as there had been no signs that something like that could possibly happen. We all came home and gathered as a family to plan and prepare for Dad's funeral. For the first time in my life, I felt like I had no idea what to do next. My world came crashing down when my dad passed away.

We learned that he had had a heart attack, which took his life suddenly. Many years of not looking after himself had brought him to his eventual fate. Not only was I shocked, but I was very disappointed with how he had left things. His relationship with Mom, his relationship with his kids, the state of his farming operation, the way the house was a mess, and many other things.

It took us nearly two years to get through all his paperwork, taxes, bills, and all the farming accounting. I spent a lot of time following his paper trail of unpaid bills to really get an understanding of why he was in the situation he was in.

I became angry and I resented the entire picture of what he had left behind for us, and more specifically, for Mom. At just two months shy of 57 years old, it seemed to me that he had left behind a life of disarray- And we were left to pick up the pieces.

My heart hurt for Mom for many years. With Dad gone, she was left at the house all by herself, all alone. To me it seemed very unfair, and these feelings would sit with me for quite some time.

I watched my mom go through complete devastation and many heartaches when my dad passed. We were left with the challenge of putting together the pieces of his life that he had left undone for so long. We did not anticipate the heartache and pain it would cause us.

Chanda's strength and ability to keep us together as a family carried us through those days and years. Getting through all the firsts like Christmas, anniversaries, and birthdays was definitely a challenge. Dad loved Christmas and had put up decorations all over the house for many years when I was a kid, so without him, Christmas was a very hard time for me.

I'm sure we all felt it at Christmas time. That's why it became even more important for us as a family to be together for holidays, birthdays, and anniversaries whenever we possibly could. Christmas remained a special time for us, even though it was probably one of the most difficult times for us as a family.

When Kamryn and Miguire came along, it was as though Christmas had new meaning. There was excitement in the air again with new little ones around the table at Christmas time. In my mind, that time of year was very difficult from the time my dad passed in 2006 until Kamryn was born in 2011. Having a new little baby in the home when we celebrated Christmas just made it that much more special. The hurt and pain had dissipated enough that we were able to enjoy it again as a family.

THE MOST AMAZING CHRISTMAS

IN THE LATE fall of 2015, plans started coming together for our family Christmas, and for the first time in many years, Chanda decided to take time off between Christmas and New Year's. This allowed us lots of time to visit with her and Jordan and the kids. Everyone knows how special Christmas can be with little kids, and 2015 was going to be just the best time ever together!

Kamryn and Miguire spent lots of time with us even when Chanda and Jordan weren't around, which allowed them to have some adult time without the kids. This worked out great for us all. Just like any other small children, they were just a little bit different when Mom and Dad were not around. We played hard, we laughed hard, and we snuggled and cuddled hard. We just spent the most incredible time together.

I remember the day that we celebrated Christmas, although I can't remember if it was the 25th or another day close to that date. That was the Christmas I gave Kamryn and Miguire the Barbie doll and the mini sticks. I still cherish those items and think about them often.

I specifically remember Miguire attempting to figure out how to shoot the little sponge ball around the house with his mini stick. At one point he accidentally hit the couch. He stopped, leaned over towards the couch, and said sorry in his sweet little voice. "Sarry…" We often say this in our daily conversations now, almost as though it is a reminder of him. It always makes me smile.

It's really evident in my life now that anything to do with small children is something that I get emotional about instantly. I'm the guy hiding in the back of the room with tears rolling off his face when I'm at a kids' Christmas concert or sporting event. I'm the guy who sometimes, in fact almost always, has tears in his eyes when there's an event of any kind involving small children. Even if it's an event that MY kids are in, I just get teary—I feel it a little bit extra. I believe this happens for two reasons. First, the thought "What if one of my kids were gone?" is always on my mind. Second, it's as though my mind instantly goes to Kamryn and Miguire and how they would be doing in that event or that scenario. I picture them in place of the other kids, enjoying experiences they would never get to have.

When I'm at Sage's hockey games and he's on the ice, quite often I think about Miguire and Kamryn watching Cousin Sage skating around on the rink playing hockey. And even that makes me sad; that Kamryn and Miguire didn't get the chance to play hockey. They didn't get the chance to feel the cold breeze rushing over their face skating down the ice. They didn't get the chance to hear the crowd cheer when they scored a goal; a chance to high five Mom and Dad when they came off the ice.

If I'm at one of Hudson's band concerts or school plays I often think about Kamryn and Miguire and how much they would have loved that kind of stuff too. They didn't have the chance to perform on stage in front of their peers at school or for their parents. They didn't have the chance to play an instrument or have the feeling of what it's like to be part of a group like band.

Now, nearly four years after the accident, I've come to think that these thoughts will always stay with me. My emotions are always at a high when I'm at any event that my kids are at. Not even just my kids—any kids. It does get better over time though, to the point that now, yes,

I still have that emotion and there still might be tears, but quite often I smile when I think about how great they would have been at sports and school. At all the things that kids get to do when growing up and how great it would have been to watch them participate. It warms my heart, and it fills me with joy when I think of those things, even though I'm still full of emotion.

I often find myself really having to make an effort to focus on my own kids when I'm out at an event that they are involved in. I don't want to miss those moments. I want to be present so that I will retain those memories of my own children. I realize that wishing other people were there takes away from the moment and affects how I feel about what's happening in that moment in time. It requires constant focus to let the emotion happen and bring myself back to the present moment in order to see it for what it is. In order to be present with my children.

I often say to my sweetheart Angie that it's annoying to have eyes full of tears or cheeks that need to be wiped. Thank goodness she tells me not to ever change that. She always assures me that that is one of the biggest reasons why she loves me. What I've learned in the last four years is that when I show emotion and don't hide it, it helps me and others in so many ways. In every way! I really do think that the way that I've navigated through the last four years has provided me with the means to direct my life in a more purposeful way. My ability to connect with people on a different level is much, much better and stronger. I am able to show others that it's ok to show emotion; that we should not try to hide it.

This approach has and continues to serve me well, even though sometimes I do find it inconvenient that I can get so super emotional. I just miss the kids so bad sometimes, but I do also realize that what happened changed me and is leading me to a different life. A life that is much more fulfilling and happy. At times I feel like I'm fully exposed when I'm emotional in a public place, but in reality, I believe that openness and emotional capacity is what is leading me to do what I am doing right now; writing this book and collaborating with Catherine and her family.

Furthermore, I believe that the more I am in touch with my emotions, the better I am able to connect with people—men in particular who have a hard time showing their emotions or connecting with their feminine side. Since the car accident, I have connected with more people on a deeper level in such a profound way that it has become who I am. I have become and I am becoming someone who has the ability to connect and relate with other people in a very deep, personal, and understanding way. This allows me to guide and teach others to get through some of life's most difficult things in a healthy way.

Christmas feels whole and complete again because of the work I have done within myself. 2015 was an amazing Christmas, and now, as I complete this portion of the book just days before Christmas 2020, with Covid-19 changing things drastically, I am having the best Christmas again! The ones in-between were less than desirable, but they were part of the healing and grieving process, and that is ok with me.

MAKING CONTACT

MIDWAY THROUGH 2018, I started thinking about contacting Catherine McKay. I was curious to see if she would be willing to have a conversation with me. I had come across a couple of her children through Facebook based on some of the posts that I had followed. I had figured out that it was them. So I knew I would have the means to reach out to them when I was ready to do so. It was on my mind to reach out and tell Catherine that I forgave her, and I wasn't sure what else might come of it. These thoughts sat in my mind for a few months before I actually got the nerve to reach out to one of her daughters.

In December 2018 I messaged Catherine‘s oldest daughter. I recall lying in bed after day one of the PSI Seminar. I was alone and left to my thoughts about things in my life that were not yet sitting well with me. This just hours after hearing the facilitator share his story about the bar he once managed and that they had served a couple of patrons who then left intoxicated and killed someone with their vehicle.

In my overwhelmed state, I was wondering just how Catherine McKay's family were doing. I knew I needed to put my thoughts into words and send a message. I was a bit apprehensive as to how she would respond and hoped very much that my message would be received openly. In fact, I finished the message off with "Please find this message with a soft heart and an open mind," as if I was trying to make my words come across in the easiest, lightest, and most caring way. I meant no harm; only love. I had no expectations, I was only sharing my thoughts. I actually wrote, "If you do not want me to ever message again, please just say so and I would understand."

At 1:21 am on December 14th, I hit send on the message that would forever change who I was and am. It would also be the start of my open communication with the McKay family in a most profound way. I fell asleep shortly after sending the message, full of curiosity as to how my words would be received and whether or not I would get a message back or not. I was pleasantly surprised with the most loving response at 8 pm the following day. With great eagerness and a heart full of kindness and care, I read and reread her reply.

In my message to Catherine's daughter, I had spoken of forgiveness and asked how she and her family were doing. I was apprehensive about the message and I really didn't know how it was going to turn out. I just knew in my heart that I was led to reach out to see if there was possibly a chance I would be able to have a conversation with Catherine at some point.

I was incredibly amazed with the response I received from Catherine's eldest daughter. It seemed as though she was delighted to hear from me and also excited that I was talking about forgiveness. She explained to me that she was having a hard time finding forgiveness towards her own mother for what she had done to my family. After messaging back and forth for about half an hour, she actually sent me a mailing address so that I could send Catherine a letter at the healing lodge where she was serving her sentence. She seemed apprehensive about giving me the mailing address and said, "It seems like you have genuine concern for my mother and I just hope you have the best interest in mind for her and for us." I could certainly understand why she would think that way.

I was putting myself in her shoes, trying my best to understand where she was coming from and why she was saying most things.

Knowing that Catherine's daughter was ok with me sending a letter seemed to give me a sense of direction. At that point, I really didn't know what I was going to write in the letter other than that I forgave her and asking whether she'd be willing to have a conversation with me. For months, those thoughts sat idle in my mind before I worked up the nerve to actually write a letter.

In June 2019, I decided it was time to write that letter to Catherine at the healing lodge. I didn't put a whole lot of thought into it. I just let the words flow from within me, speaking out my forgiveness and also telling her that I wanted to collaborate with her to share our stories. The day I dropped the letter in the mailbox, I really had a feeling that I was doing exactly what I was supposed to be doing. Something was calling me to do this.

In July of the same year, I arranged to have a meeting with Catherine‘s second eldest daughter, Kayla. We met at a local coffee shop in the town that she lives in, and we had an amazing two-hour conversation. It was super emotional and raw. We shared our thoughts and our feelings, and we were truly engaged in a heartfelt conversation. She must have said sorry a few hundred times. Every time I looked her in the eyes and said, "It's not your fault, you have nothing to be sorry for." For at least the first hour there were tears flowing from one of our faces or both as we shared very, very real things from our lives.

At times, we ended up holding hands across the table as if to console one another. It was the most humbling experience I had had for quite some time. She talked about her mom and shared with me what kind of a person she had been before the accident. I sensed really quickly that her mom was her hero and her best friend.

Kayla shared many different stories about her mom with me that day. All of the stories painted a picture of Catherine caring for kids in her community and in her neighborhood for many years. I had visions in my head of a close-knit family, with her mom taking in all the neighborhood kids as well as all of her children's friends. They were all welcome at the house at any time. Catherine sure sounded like a woman who had a very caring heart and always went out of her way to make sure everybody was looked after.

Our open chat about our loved ones naturally progressed to my sharing with Kayla how close my relationship with Chanda had been. I conveyed that she had been my best friend and my go-to person nearly every single day. Yet I paused when I spoke of Kamryn and Miguire, as I sensed Kayla's emotions were at a boiling point when it came to talking about the kids. Purposefully, I allowed her to share about her family more than I did about mine. It was what needed to happen.

I remember thinking in that coffee shop that day that our conversation was not in any way awkward or strange. It just happened. It was needed. It was as though the two of us needed to sit down and talk to each other eye to eye and touch hands. To really share how hurt and devastated we were and to console one another. When she walked through the door and we both extended hands to shake, it was more than that. The hug that followed the handshake indicated that we were both very willing to be open and vulnerable.

At the end of our amazing first meeting, we parted ways with a wonderful warm hug. The tears had turned into bright and hopeful smiles; the shaking and trembling hands had steadied.

I walked out of the coffee shop and across the street to my parked car, and the very second that I opened the door and got into the car, the tears started flowing uncontrollably. But they were different tears—tears of hope, tears of calmness, and tears of joy. I was overwhelmed with a sense of understanding. I really felt like what had just happened was exactly what was supposed to happen.

When we were in the coffee shop, Kayla shared a letter with me that her mother Catherine had sent to her. In it, Catherine had responded to the letter I had written to her. She communicated with me through her daughter Kayla in the most amazing way. She wrote, "Chad and I are going to change the world." She was happy with the things I had written in my letter and was more than willing to talk about it all and collaborate with me in any way she could.

The most amazing thing I learned from that letter was that Catherine had run a marathon in the healing lodge, and in 2017, 2018, and 2019, she had run a half marathon every year. I was pleasantly surprised to learn this considering the fact that I had also run a marathon in 2019 to raise money for MADD (Mothers Against Drunk Driving). Catherine gathered donations from fellow inmates, prison guards, and the like to raise money for MADD. Amazingly, the coincidences and synchronicities seemed to be lining up.

Three years earlier, I heard her saying in her court statement that she would spend the rest of her life making a difference in the world and preventing this from happening to other families. So when I learned that she was running marathons and contributing to MADD, I was incredibly delighted.

That day in July after meeting with Kayla, I realized that we would need to share our conversations. I knew that other people had to hear our conversations, feel our conversations, understand our conversations, and really have a sense for what we were talking about. The drive home that night was two and a half hours, and the entire drive all I could think about was that I needed to share this with the world.

Over the previous 10 years I had jokingly said many times that I should write a book about my life. That warm summer night in July was the first time I actually thought that the book idea could be something real. The letter that Catherine had written to Kayla was with me in the car on the way home. I thought about what to do most of the way home. What was next? How would I do this?

Perhaps the toughest part for me was hearing how difficult it had been for Kayla and her siblings during the period of time when their mother was in prison for killing four people. She shared with me how "other people that knew me and also ones that didn't know me and my siblings were saying just the nastiest and meanest things to me and my family." They called them all kinds of demeaning names, coming from a place of hatred, anger, and rage. I had been wondering about those things for quite some time. What had it been like for them when their mom went away to prison? Did they have support? Were people reaching out to them in a positive way? There were so many things I was curious about.

Within an hour of leaving the coffee shop, I knew that I needed to share their story with the world. It became my duty to make sure others understood how they felt and what they went through, as well as how my family felt and what we went through. I just became overwhelmed with emotions, and it led me to believe that this was something I had to do.

For two months I had these thoughts and feelings bouncing around in my head. I considered what a book like that would be like and also considered the fact that I'd never been an author before. Even then, the feeling that I had to write a book just became stronger and stronger as time passed. In September 2019, when I was at a personal development event, we were asked to write down a goal on a piece of paper that we felt we needed to accomplish in our life. Within two weeks, I had started writing my book.

MA'S MAFIA

THROUGH MESSAGING AND face-to-face conversations, I have learned a little bit about who Catherine was before the tragedy occurred from her family. I have heard them talk about how kind and caring she was to everybody around her, including strangers.

Catherine's home was a home where everyone was welcome. She created an environment that was a safe place to be and a place to go if you needed help. Meeting face-to-face with Spencer, Kayla, Parker, and their eldest sister has really given me a sense of who Catherine really was.

While at Spencer's house, I heard stories of get-togethers where music was always to be heard. Catherine's musical ability and talents were showcased at many of these parties or get-togethers. There were lots of laughs and fun to be had by anybody that was welcomed into the home. The eldest of the siblings left home at an early age, while the others stayed long enough to graduate high school.

The siblings told me stories about how people who needed refuge or were in trouble with addictions—or possibly with the law—came to see

Catherine to seek a place of safety, to get some advice, or just a hot meal and respite from the cruel world that was out there.

I quickly got the sense that Catherine was always looking out for everybody else around her, supporting them in any way she possibly could. In doing so, she created a bit of a following with local people who knew she had their back. And in return, they had hers.

At times, people would come to the house looking for somebody or possibly to threaten people who may have been in the house or were there at one time. Catherine, with her big heart and kind, caring personality, always saw the best in people, and she would always look out for them. So when trouble came knocking at the door, she always did her best to defuse the situation while protecting the best interest of everybody involved.

The term Ma's Mafia was coined back in those days to describe Catherine's following—a group of people who were attempting to be the best versions of themselves. They were creating a circle of influence of people that were making a difference in the world and helping others. Catherine would often be found sitting at the kitchen table helping someone achieve their GED or complete a resume or job application. She was always leading others in the right direction and helping them better themselves.

A full-grown man even a foot taller than Catherine stood no chance when it came to her standing up for her people and for the things that she believed to be right. This included people that were struggling with alcohol and /or drugs. She would do her best to help them get clean and sober.

At times, people would try to bring drugs into her home, and she would have nothing of it. She made sure that everybody knew they would not be welcome in her home if drugs were found on them. People just knew that it was a place they could go to try to straighten out or get help.

With pride, Catherine's children shared just how much their mom truly cared for people, even when they did things that were less than perfect. She still saw the good in them, always making an effort to steer them the right way in life. To better themselves.

For most of their lives, Catherine's children grew up with alcohol in the home as a norm. They had to navigate their way through school and their personal lives while dealing with alcoholism. Some of them partied hard and some of them partied just a little, in the end always knowing that their mom cared dearly for them and their friends.

In one particular conversation, Spencer shared stories with me of times when fights would break out and his mom would get in-between two fully grown men to break it up. These fully grown men knew and respected Catherine, and they knew that she would definitely stand her ground. Whatever Mama said is what went. She was the boss of the home, and anyone that spent time there knew it. There was a mutual respect between people visiting the family home and Catherine and her children.

On several occasions, Catherine's children told me stories of her taking away keys from people who had had too many drinks or possibly drugs. She absolutely did not allow anyone to drink and drive after they had been at her home for parties or get-togethers.

I very quickly learned that Catherine's children idolized her. They told me more than once that she was their hero. I listened to them talk about her and share stories, full of pride and joy. They painted a vivid picture for me of someone that they held in very high regard and who had a very special place in their hearts and souls.

Growing up and living in Buffalo Narrows was rough for Catherine and her five kids in the early years. Having very little time with their dad proved to be a challenge, yet they persevered and enjoyed rewarding times as well.

Each time I speak to Catherine's children, I get a better sense of who she really was and I believe still is. I really believe that somebody who used to be like that would still be the same. So kind, caring, and giving. Someone who was and is willing to give the shirt off her back to anybody that needs it. Although I wasn't sure, I suspected this was the case early on, when I first heard Catherine speak in court in July 2016 about spending the rest of her life preventing this from happening to other families. Those words are still with me and always will be.

Hearing Spenny and his siblings speak about their mom and how hard it is to not see her and talk to her like they used to touches my heart in a different way than anything else I've ever heard. The talks I had with them became about more than just writing a book and gathering information. It became about me wanting to speak to Catherine's children to see how they were doing. It's an indescribable feeling, the connection I feel with them; tender and hurting hearts able to communicate and connect on a very deep, personal level.

I hope to one day meet Catherine and have that connection carry on in a very profound way. Somehow, the combination of all these efforts are coming together for a higher purpose. I believe that one day Catherine and I will collaborate on something much bigger. That day in court she resolved to spend the rest of her life helping to prevent this from happening to other families. It seems as though that is the direction my heart and soul are leading me in as well.

The one letter that I wrote to Catherine that she responded to through her daughter showed me that she still has the same intent as she did four years ago. I was happy to hear that and that she supports what I'm doing as well. This excites me and really allows me to go forward with what I'm doing. It's great that most of Catherine's children speak to me and share their stories, and it's even better that Catherine is willing to share a few things as well.

Despite the fact that some people think what I'm doing is something they would be unable to do, I still push forward knowing that this is what I am meant to do. Chanda is up there forever pushing me and guiding me; I can feel it every step of the way. I know she's there. In fact, I know all four of them are there, always pushing me forward.

Many years ago, I was told that finding a dime on the ground is a whisper or a message from a loved one that has passed away. It has been remarkable how many times I have found dimes on the ground. In fact, occasionally four at a time. I choose to smile and believe that my four angels above are looking down on me and sending me little messages here and there, just to remind me that I am on the right path and doing the right things.

Almost daily I ask myself, what would Chanda say or do in this situation? On days when I am feeling good and things are seemingly going very well, I know she would be smiling with pride. And in a way, she keeps me in check. Chanda would always do what was right, and I live by that principle daily. So much so that there are times when it does not make sense to do the things I am doing, but it is what feels right. Every day I am grateful for who Chanda was and still is.

The very first time I met Kayla in the coffee shop and we shared our thoughts, feelings, and stories, it was clear that her heart was broken, just like mine. We had an instant connection.

My first meeting with Spenny, Parker, and their eldest sister was no different. I believe that being open, honest, and vulnerable with one another allowed us all to know our hearts were all hurting in a very similar way. Even after some time has gone by, the hurt is still there.

It's a very surreal feeling, the feeling that we are healing together. I fully believe that our conversations and meetings are meant to happen. I know I come away from them feeling just a little better than I did before, and I know the feeling is mutual.

Some really great things can come even from such tragedy. Perhaps it might seem odd to some. But I feel as though I have gained some very close friends; perhaps even more than that—new family.

Our conversations have gone beyond just putting a book together to share stories about how this has all impacted us. As I write this today, I would say that this is much bigger than just a book and that our conversations will carry on for quite some time going forward. I think we have forged lifelong connections.

I can only close my eyes and imagine how these conversations will carry on once Catherine is a part of them. Particularly face-to-face, when we will be able to read the emotion on each other's faces. I often think about that first meeting; what might be said or what it might feel like. I just know that it's going to be very profound and very positive. A continuation of healing hearts.

With a smile, I wonder if Ma's Mafia would welcome the new guy with open arms and hearts like they used to back in the day. I feel as though I am part of it just from the stories and connections that have been made.

CATHERINE'S SONS: SPENNY AND PARKER

ON THE DAY of the accident, Kayla phoned both her brothers to tell them what had happened. "Something's happened to Mom."

Spenny told me that his first question was, "Is she dead?"

Many other questions raced through the brothers' minds. Was everyone ok? Had people died? Was Mom ok? Who caused this? Before dinner at Spenny's house, Catherine's sons candidly shared with me how hard it had been to hear about the accident and its tragic results.

As brothers do, they were ribbing each other back and forth a little as we all shared our experiences of January 2016. Spenny shared that he "hit the bottle" for about six months after the accident. He found it hard to deal with what had happened with his mom, as well as the after effects of others being so harsh towards him and his family. He told me that it was not uncommon for him to go to the bar, have a few drinks, and then pick fights with anyone and everyone in an attempt to find a release for his anger.

After some time, boxing became his healthy escape from the drinking. It helped bring him some peace. "Boxing three times a week, then four, then five; just to keep my mind busy in a healthy way."

Parker shared that he too was "checked out of life" for some of 2016. After his mom went to prison, he didn't know how to go on living a normal life.

It was great to hear the two banter back and forth about some of their memories as youngsters. Spenny would sometimes beat on his little brother Parker, only to face the wrath of his eldest brother Danny. It sounded to me like any other household where boys fought and wrestled as they grew up. They both laughed as they told me about a time Spenny had accidently knocked out Parker's tooth with a mini stick.

The two explained how hard it was to see the things posted on social media about how their mom should die. How all their families should die. Catherine's kids and grandkids should all be dead. They both spoke of taking time off social media to get away from the harsh comments, such as "Your mom is a monster and you should all die." These words angered me. I had a hard time understanding why people felt it was ok to trash talk Spenny and his siblings, when in fact they had done nothing wrong.

It was great to share our thoughts and feelings, especially with the amazing smell of supper cooking in the house—pulled pork, only it was really elk. Nickolas (Spenny's son) was sitting in his high chair eating Cheerios. He and I got to know each other just a little that day, and it was so heartwarming.

I was sitting on Spenny's couch in complete awe. How was I there talking to Catherine's two boys about life? About normal things? As if we had known each other for years. We talked about our memories from when we were kids. "Pointless things," Parker called them. Funny how we can remember silly things we did as kids, yet as adults, our memories seem to fail us daily. We all chuckled over that more than once.

Little man Nickolas, who was running around in his diaper each time I had the chance to hang out at Spenny's house, captured my heart every single time. At 18 months old or so, he would attempt to form words while keeping his mouth closed, managing only little mumbles and lots of pointing with his adorable little fingers to get what he needed.

We talked about work, school, friends, and the like as the conversation unfolded. The two brothers spoke to me about Buffalo Narrows and Ile-A-La-Crosse. That had been their home back in the days when their mom was still around.

At one point I asked what it would be like when their mom is out of the healing lodge. Without hesitation, Spenny said, "Awkward. It will at least be easier to see her." He shared that at least he and his family would only need to travel a few hours from home to see her again. He figured it would be awkward to see her again, and talking to her would be very different than it had been before. That said, there was definitely some excitement in his voice when he was talking about being able to call and see his mom whenever he wanted.

Catherine not having a driver's license or a vehicle would prove to be a challenge as well. Spenny had lived very close to his mom for most of his life up until she was incarcerated. He only needed to walk a few blocks to see her back when they lived in Buffalo Narrows. The new normal would be much different; they would be almost three hours apart, and she would not have a driver's license.

Spenny has been granted visitation rights to see his mom at the Healing Lodge. But having kids, it isn't all that easy to go, and there are strict rules to follow while there, some of which he has a tough time making happen.

He shared that Catherine once got a one-day pass to head to a location near Saskatoon, where Spenny, his wife, and kids were able to see her for a few hours. Catherine's boyfriend was there as well. Catherine and Spenny had spent some time cuddling on the couch, cherishing the moments as they talked about friends and family.

Spenny said that the toughest moment that day was saying goodbye again. It was the very first time Catherine had met her grandson Nickolas, who was walking and roughing around. Spenny could see the look on his mom's face, and he knew it was a "kick to her face that she missed out on so many things."

"I tried my hardest not to cry as I looked out the window when we drove away," Catherine's son said with obvious emotion in his voice.

Spenny said that his mom has been denied other visitations and day passes. He believes that someone in our extended family finds out about them and makes all efforts to stop them from happening. Sometimes they are canceled just the day before.

Together we chatted about what it would be like for me to sit next to their mom, establishing a little bit of trust and boundaries. Perhaps there would be awkward silence. Would we have to lay out some ground rules? Would we cry or break down? It was impossible to say.

Again the brothers talked of their family home being a safe home; a place for people young and old to go to for guidance or assistance—help with all things in life. People struggling with addictions or alcohol, relationships, school, or anything else were welcome. Although there were frequent parties at the family home, it was always a place of safety and support.

Being the youngest, Parker would "just hide in the basement to stay away from it all." That's where his bedroom was. School was important to Parker; he wanted to finish strong and graduate high school.

Later in our visit, Spenny's wife Frankie returned home from work and shared details of her Monday. It was great to see her again for a short visit before I left. Her little man was excited to see her come through the door, just like any toddler does when a parent comes home from work. This again filled my heart with warmth and appreciation for being a part of their day.

After three hours or so, I was on my way. I was again in awe about how comfortable Spenny and I were with each other. It was my first time meeting Parker, and I would say he was a little more reserved and quiet than Spenny. I look forward to meeting all of them again.

As I drove away that day, I could not help but smile. I believe we all gained some valuable healing and understanding from that afternoon's conversation.

KAYLA AT THE BAKERY FOR THE SECOND TIME

KAYLA AND I met at the bakery again for our second face-to-face meeting. I wanted to find out how things were going with her and her family. I was hoping for another great conversation, and I wasn't disappointed.

Her baby son, Samuel, was at home sleeping. Kayla said she was tired because her little guy had kept her awake most the night.

She mentioned that her eldest son was almost the same age that Miguire would have been if he were still alive. It was very hard for her to know that her mom had taken the lives of two kids so close to the age of her own kids.

Kayla had talked to her mom just the day before and told her that she and I were meeting to talk about the book and about life. Catherine had shared her frustrations with restorative justice and how she wished she could respond to my letter directly. She said that she would love to communicate back and forth with me, even if it was through Kayla for now. I was happy to hear that she was still willing to do so.

Kayla and I spoke of my kids and hers, of life in general, of her husband and his carpenter job, the economy, and most importantly, how it was going with her little man, who was just two months old to the day.

When I asked her how she had been since we last spoke, she replied with a heartfelt, "I just don't know how you can forgive. You are a stronger person than I am." She couldn't believe that I wanted to talk to her and her family, particularly her mom.

She told me that she was still having a very hard time forgiving her mom. "Spenny maybe doesn't understand fully how hard this is for her and me," she said. "He wasn't in court to hear five hours of victim statements being read." The emotion in her voice really showed how hard it had been for her to hear about me and my family's devastation. It was very apparent that those words were still really tugging on her heartstrings.

We chatted about driving and how we think or worry about getting in an accident. How we make sure to buckle the kids in extra tight, and all the worries and concerns driving down the highway.

She brought something up that I hadn't thought of before. She wondered if, in that instant her mom's Jeep met Chanda and Jordan's car, there was a split second to look back at the kids as the car was being smashed. Was Chanda able to have one last glance at her kids sleeping in the back, just for a second?

After giving it some thought, I became certain there hadn't been time for that to happen. In my mind it was instant. They were gone immediately. As a mom, it makes sense that Kayla would want there to be time to look back at her kids if she was ever in a similar situation. Just one last glance at her littles!

Catherine's youngest daughter also shared a little more around her thoughts on drinking and driving in our society and how it's socially acceptable for people to have a couple and drive. "How can we change that?" she asked." Is there a way to change how we view that as a whole?"

Some parts of our conversation that day were much the same as our first conversation. It was intellectual and emotional, and so good. Two people so very much on the same page. "It can't happen to me," was said multiple times.

"My mom isn't a heartless human being," Kayla said. "I can't imagine what it was like for Mom to wake up in a jail cell and learn she killed a family that mirrored your children's family." I nodded in agreement. "I would just want to die," Kayla said. "I got the call Mom was involved in an accident and that people are dead. Immediately I thought, 'Mom is dead.' I was sick, literally sick to my stomach."

The initial shock had her reeling. She needed to talk to her mom, so she got in her vehicle and drove to Saskatoon. "I have to find my mom. I have to see her and talk to her. Where is she?" Again, I could hear the anguish and hurt in Kayla's voice.

She told me that they didn't know what was happening for nearly a full day. So many questions and so few answers. It was unsettling and heart wrenching. "What do we do, where do we go?"

In the early evening that day in 2016 Kayla learned more. "Mom was in jail and had killed four people!" She was shocked and devastated. "How fucking dare you?! You should be the one dead." She couldn't understand how this could possibly be happening when her mom was always the one who did good. "Everything mom did that was good was erased that day." I listened full of pure emotion, as I just could not imagine how she must have felt hearing such horrible news.

In an attempt to possibly steer the conversation away from such an emotional time, Kayla then shared a little about her mom at the healing lodge. "Mushum, the native grandfather Mom has at the healing lodge, treats her well and works closely with her." Kayla shared that her mom was happy to have the amazing support of her Mushum.

She also spoke of the Van De Vorsts and their anger towards her mom. She understood "how hard it would be to forgive someone if they took her kids' lives, leaving chairs empty at the supper table." She again said that she found my strength and ability to heal remarkable.

Our amazing conversation ended there, as Kayla knew her precious baby would be getting very hungry by then. Just like the previous time, we parted ways with hugs, smiles, and well wishes for one another before going on with our days. I again left there with an amazing sense of peace and love. Yes, it is possible to love another family that is directly related to the woman that took some of my family away. It felt so good to love and accept.

CHECKED OUT TO COME BACK

AT SOME POINT near the end of 2016, I began to think a little bit differently. My short-term memory was coming back, and my mental clarity was also a little more intact. Running multiple businesses in 2016 with very little mental capacity to do so was more than a challenge. My road repair business is a seasonal business that shuts down in October when the weather gets cool, and I really felt like I was not there mentally or emotionally for the entire season.

I knew that financially I was in trouble. I had checked out of life and work for nearly a year. The million dollar business I ran in 2015 became half of that in 2016, and the financial stressors were mounting.

In November or December of 2016, I knew I had a choice. I had a choice to give up or to fully believe that I could still make all this work. So every morning when I got up, I made a conscious decision to believe that everything that I had started businesswise was still something that I could make happen and succeed in.

During the winters of 2016 and 2017, I put my mind to work building my business in the belief that the next season was going to be another million-dollar year for road repair. I also started exploring my plans for

Napa Auto Parts, which had been put on hold for nearly a year. I had started the plans to build a greenfield Napa Auto Parts in 2015 with the intention of building in 2016, however that did not happen once the accident occurred; it was just too much. In March 2017, the engineering drawings for Napa were complete. I finally started feeling like my mind was running on all cylinders and that the businessman in me was back.

In the summer of 2017, my road repair business performed halfway between the amazing success of 2015 and the horrible year of 2016. I was happy with the outcome, considering what the year before had brought. We broke ground on the brand-new Napa store, and the building went up by the fall of 2017. We were planning to open the store in December of that year. With hard work and determination, we made it happen.

With pride, we opened the store on December 7th with Tana, my mom, and myself as partners. The amazing thing with this project is that it's more than just a building and a business. The three of us used the funds from Chanda and Jordan's estate to put the deal together. Their legacy became our business. Every day I step foot in that building I'm reminded of the four angels that helped make it happen. It fills me with pride knowing that Chanda, Jordan, and the kids will make an impact on the town in which Chanda grew up.

Running multiple businesses while grieving and healing was and is incredibly challenging to do. I could go into further details, yet I feel it is unimportant.

As I write this book in January 2020, the financial burden weighs very heavily on my shoulders. Again I ask myself what I believe and what I see happening in the future. Now more than ever, I'm leaning into faith and the belief that somehow this all will work out, even though I have no idea how.

I have done a tremendous amount of personal development work in the last four years to help me through the tough times. I honestly and truly believe that I have grown in leaps and bounds mentally, emotionally, and spiritually, and that I'm stronger than ever. The question is, how will the financial end play out?

In my heart, I know that losing four angels to a drunk driver has had a massive impact on me and has definitely played a part in the situation I am in. I also know that it has changed me 100%, and for the better. I am growing into the best version of me. Businesses that once excited me very, very much do not seem to do so any longer. Would that be different if there was no financial burden riding so heavily on my shoulders? Time will tell…

I do know one thing for sure. Writing this book and being in contact with Catherine's children, and even with Catherine, is absolutely what I'm supposed to be doing. Without a doubt, this is the direction I am going in; this is who I am now. Sharing my story on social media has shown me even more that this is absolutely what I NEED to be doing.

I strongly believe that once I moved from the financial, business-minded Chad and into the heart-centered, caring Chad, things shifted for me. I started to put more thought into my daily connections with other people in my life, with the understanding that the business and finances would follow.

Heading into 2017, I came to the realization at some point that I had to think about this in a different way. That it was up to me to figure out a way to get out of the hole that I had fallen into. To recover and to get back on my feet.

A time came when the sad songs I had been listening to were starting to sound different to me in a way that is indescribable. It was as though they somehow were bringing me peace and joy rather than the sadness and sorrow I was accustomed to. Just the same, food that had very little taste for quite some time started to actually taste good and feel amazing to experience. I cannot pinpoint a certain day, week, or even a month when this all started to change, however, I do know that it was great to have it happening. Once I started getting these little glimpses of hope that I was repairing, that I was improving mentally and emotionally, I knew I had to find ways to keep that going. I had to figure out a way to have the feel-good moments stay for minutes, and then those minutes would turn into hours.

I knew I had to consciously work towards this daily. To find joy in my favorite things again rather than sinking in sorrow and sadness. The hurt and pain needed to be flushed out with joy and happiness in order for me to be ME again.

I began waking up in the morning each and every day thinking that this is all going to work out and that this is all repairable. The businesses that hadn't run themselves in 2016 when I was grieving would recover now that I was back. My mind was set on having a great 2017. It had to be in order for things to get back to where they were in 2015 before the accident.

One day, I found myself at my father's graveside. I honestly had no idea why I was there; I really didn't stop there often.. I had been holding on to anger for 10 years, and I was really struggling to figure out why I was so disappointed, angry, and mad at my dad. On this day, something was different. I felt like my shoulders were a little bit lighter, almost as though I was starting to understand who he was, and more importantly, how he saw things in the world that I didn't understand at the time.

That cool fall day, something profound changed in me. I started to really appreciate the positive things about my dad and who he was. I think I connected with his heart; his healing heart. The man was full of so many great things, and up until that day, there had been a fog in my mind around those things. I had been focused on all the things I didn't like about him for so long; the things I felt he didn't do right. Sitting there on the grass with my knees crossed, I spoke some words that I hadn't said ever in my life. I said, "Dad, I forgive you." The tears started flowing. My blood was pumping fast, and I thought my head started to find clarity.

It was the most amazing feeling I had that afternoon while visiting with my father at his grave. The crisp, cool air blowing in my face reminded me that it was the coldest time of the day. Things were changing inside of me. I was changing. I was accepting the way things had been and still were. Even though I didn't like everything about my dad, from that day forward I was focused solely on the things I did like. It was an incredible feeling. As soon as I vocalized the word "forgive", it was as though I became 100 pounds lighter.

The days to follow seemed to go the same way as I talked to people in a different frame of mind. I tried to always see the good while still understanding the not so good and accepting it. Thoughts of Catherine McKay and who she really was started to go through my mind on a daily basis. I started to really wonder how she had ended up in a car going 105 km per hour, killing four innocent people. As horrible as that act had been, where could the good be found? Was Catherine still filled with thoughts of preventing this from happening to other families? Was she still true to her word as she declared in her court statement in July 2016?

I found myself contemplating what Catherine was doing while in prison and what she would do when she got out. Would she make a difference in this world and be a contributor? Would she truly make a difference and prevent this from happening to other families? Or would she go back on her word and break her promises? Does she feel remorse? What does she think every day? How does she feel when she wakes up in the morning—or does she even sleep?

Working through all these thoughts and questions in my own mind landed me in a place of forgiveness very quickly. I recall wondering one day, with a massive grin on my face, how it could possibly have taken me 10 years to forgive my dad and only months to forgive Catherine McKay. What I really came to understand at that time was that the pain and suffering I had caused myself by hanging on to anger and resentment towards my father would only be 1000 times worse if I did the same with Catherine. I came to the realization that I couldn't do that. It would eat me alive.

I've sat down to write this letter more times than I can count. There is so much going through my mind that I'm not sure where to start. As we move into the holidays and the second anniversary of our life changing events I can't help but finally write to you.

January 4, 2016.....a day neither of us will soon ever forget. At 1:30 in the morning we got a phone call that forever changed our lives. A call I never thought we would get. They had a heart for our son.

As we spoke to the flight crew and went over the particulars of how long we had until we needed to be at the airport, I couldn't help but think of what this meant for another family who's life was changing forever in a different way. It is very bittersweet to understand what happens when a life is saved by organ donation.

Our son who had just turned 7 years old a couple months before his heart transplant was dying. He had told me a couple weeks before that he was tired of fighting, his body felt too weak and he just wanted to quit. He had no energy to play, run, even walking was difficult as he could only go a block or so before having to stop for a break.

He was born with a Congenital Heart Defect known as Hypo-Plastic Left Heart Syndrome (HLHS). He had his first open heart surgery at 13 days old. Between then and his 3rd birthday he had 4 more. He was always blueish in colour, cold to the touch, and sweaty from his heart working so hard. Transplant was never at the top of our list of options, however after his 5th operation he developed complications. His team of doctors were able to stabilize him with medication and he lead a fairly normal life. He was doing so well in fact that we were able to ween him off the medication and he was stable still for about 1.5 years without any concerns.

In February of 2015 the complication he'd developed previously came back, and this time with a vengeance. The medication did not work as it had the first time and he quickly went downhill. We had to start taking him to the hospital every 1-3 weeks for a 4 hour long treatment that helped sustain his body. August 31, 2015 is when the doctors sat us down and told us he would need to be listed on the heart transplant list since the medications were not helping and his body would slowly shut down more and more even with the treatments he was receiving. After many tests to make sure his other organs could handle such a big surgery he was put on the heart transplant list.

The time spent on this list was nerve-racking, stressful and one of the most terrifying few months of our lives. He missed school, birthdays, he was especially sick on Christmas day that year and hardly had any energy to open his gifts.

Then just like that, there was hope. There was a second chance at life. There was health. Something we thought we would never see.

He made it through his 6th open heart surgery with flying colours. He spent the least amount of time in the hospital recovering afterward than he had with any of his other surgeries, except for one. The first time I saw him will be burned into my memory forever. He was pink!! He was warm to the touch!! The amount of oxygen in his blood was perfect, instead of always 20% too low.

He made it out of the hospital and back home in 5 weeks. We were always told it would be 2-3 months before he made it home. The amount of energy he had (and still has) is amazing! He is now one of the fastest runners in his class. He can keep up to his younger brother when they play, race, ride bikes, or rough house! He can actually make it long distances of walking without become tired in the first 10 minutes. He no longer needs to take a break in Phys. Ed.

There are no words I can say that will bring your loved family member back. I can however tell you our story, and how much our lives have changed because of the most precious life changing gift your family chose to give.

I am truly sorry for your loss. I want you to know that we will make the best of this second life he has been given. To take him on adventures and to see as much of the world as possible; because he wouldn't be here without you. I wish I could send you pictures of him to show how far he has come, so you can see what a difference your gift has made.

Thank you from the most grateful mom in the world,

I need to add a little story for you. While he was still being followed by the doctors very closely but out of the hospital and not home yet....we were taking a drive and had stopped at a store. While he and I were waiting for his dad to come back out he told me his hands were burning. I asked what he meant so I could determine if it was something to be concerned about. He again said his hands felt like they were burning and really hot. So I felt them...his hands were WARM!! He had never had warm hands before in his life and thought they were burning! I cried. There was nothing else I could do.

Ok, another one for you....We were going for a walk once we got home at a place we had been to so many times before. Our son had never made it on this walk without getting tired, needing to stop numerous times, or having us pull him in a wagon or carry him. It was only 2 months after his transplant (incredible that we were even home), and going for this walk this time he RAN (off and on) half the way and walked the other half......there were absolutely NO breaks needed, he NEVER ran out of breathe. He even beat his brother in a race!!! It was another one of the most amazing things I have witnessed in this journey. There have been so many moments like this along the way that it still blows my mind to see him do normal kid things I never thought he'd be able to do, or live to do.

He is a new kid. So full of life and adventure.

FINDING FORGIVENESS

AS I STARTED seeing the good things that had happened in 2016 rather than only the horrible, tragic, and unforgettable things, I began to make sense of it in my own head and in my inner self. I knew then that all the good things my father had been for me and my family was who I was becoming. Furthermore, I wanted to understand Catherine better. I wanted to understand who she was and all the good things that she was doing or had done in her life. I had to know more. I just had this feeling that she likely had a lot of things in common with my father, and also with me.

I also started reflecting on my own life and some of the things that I'd done. I really started examining all the things that I perceived to be negative in my life. It was a remarkable thing that once I was able to forgive my father, I also navigated my way through forgiveness for Catherine McKay as well as myself. Just exactly in what order I am not sure; there were certainly things happening simultaneously.

Every single person on this planet has done things they are not proud of. And every single person on this planet has somebody in their life that has done something to them that they are not able to forgive.

Not able to forget. I certainly have done things in my life that I'm not proud of at all, and some of those things caused very deep wounds that never healed; things I still think about. Perhaps not every day or week, but on occasion they are at the forefront of my mind. Some of them were very, very small things, while others were bigger things that I wish I would have done differently. I beat myself up over those things for quite some time.

It seemed as though I had undergone a complete shift within myself in a matter of weeks or just a few months. I became accepting of everything that has happened in my life. Each day became about asking, what good can come from this? With EVERYTHING!

The things that had happened to me in my life now became lessons. Things that I felt I had done wrong became solid stepping-stones. How can I be better now? What can I learn from my mistakes? I resolved to be better every day than I was the day before.

I had the sense that forgiving allowed me to start over in every single area of my life. I can be a better father, and I can make up for the things that I haven't done the way that I should have. I can be a better spouse for a future partner and not make the same mistakes that I've made in the past. I can be a better sibling, employee, employer, confidant, coach, everything!

There certainly was a sense of peace that came over me. I started to sleep better, eat better, think with more clarity, and be more present on a daily basis. On occasion I thought it was crazy that it took losing four of my favorite people to finally come to peace with losing my dad 10 years earlier. I also came to realize that what had happened was changing my entire being. I felt like I was becoming somebody totally different.

I had read more than once of people having a reawakening experience or a day where suddenly everything changed for them. And let me tell you, I felt like that was happening to me. It was like someone had turned on the lights and lit up the things I was missing in life. For goodness sake, how can the grass and trees just get greener and more vibrant overnight? I do not know how, I just know they did. It was incredible how my mind and eyes were just picking up things both visually and mentally like never before. Some of those things were lost for a year or two, while others were never really there at all before.

Even conversations were landing differently with me. I understood other people and myself better and with renewed excitement. I regained trust in myself as well as in others. Peaceful experiences that had passed me by in the past were becoming more apparent to me. Seeing the world and all its wonders through brighter and sharper observations had me in awe.

Some days I found myself in a trance; peaceful, connected bliss. I took extra time to see things in a new way. In essence, I was slowing down to take more in. It was what my mind needed; my soul was refueling. I was regaining ME in a big and profound way.

I believe that the old me died the same day that Chanda, Jordan, Kamryn, and Miguire died. In 2016, I was grieving the loss of four of my favorite people, in fact, I would say six of my favorite people. I was finally able to grieve the loss of my father and the loss of my previous self. I chose to be the better me. The new me.

I remember seeing a post once on social media that read, "What others think of you is none of your business." Reading those words, I chuckled to myself. For so long I had this perception of my father that wasn't necessarily true. It didn't really matter. My perception of him had zero validity, just like my perception of Catherine McKay had no validity. In fact, the perception I had of myself had no validity either.

It was an incredibly relieving feeling, knowing that I no longer cared about what anybody thought about me, nor did I care about my false perceptions of other people. I can't possibly judge somebody else if I've never walked in their shoes. I can't possibly begin to understand who they really are and why they do the things they do. Just like nobody else can judge me for the things that I've done when in fact they have never walked in my shoes. FORGIVENESS HAPPENED WHEN JUDGMENT WAS DROPPED. ACCEPTANCE HAPPENED ONCE I FORGAVE. ONCE I ACCEPTED ALL THE EVENTS THAT HAD HAPPENED IN MY LIFE, I CAME TO AN INCREDIBLE PLACE OF PEACE.

While this was all happening in the summer and fall of 2016, I went to the scene of the accident multiple times. To my knowledge, no one in the Mierau family had been at the scene of the accident nor wanted to go there. The very first time I went, I remember sitting in the ditch looking at the car parts strewn everywhere. I just sat there, crying. There were flowers taped to the light post on the corner where the accident happened, so I knew other people had stopped by. Other times I was there, there were glow sticks taped to the same light post. It warmed my heart seeing those things and knowing that other people were stopping to pay their respects, say their hellos, talk to four people gone too soon, or perhaps to make sense of what had happened.

The second time I was there I was surprised that there were still so many pieces of debris left from the vehicles. The windshield from Jordan and Chanda's car was in the cat tails in the ditch, and I picked it up and put it in the back of my truck. My intention was to only pick up the bigger pieces. I ended up picking up pieces of all shapes and sizes for about an hour. No tears, just thoughts. Remembering them, thinking about them, laughing and talking out loud.

Two of the items that I picked up went into the front of the truck. I wanted to keep them. I didn't know why, I just felt like I wanted to hang onto them, at least for the time being. One of them was Jordan's driver's license, which was still stuck in the plastic piece from the glove box. The other item was the Toyota emblem from the front of Catherine McKay's car. I simply could not fathom how the emblem was in one piece with only a few scratches.

When I got home that day, I hung the Toyota emblem on the wall in my office. No one asked me questions about it. I don't even know if anyone even saw it. For the first few days, I had to question my own sanity as to why I would hang it on the wall as a constant reminder of what had happened. It seems impossible that the emblem on the front of a car that hit another vehicle going 105 km an hour could survive—yet it did. I decided that the emblem resembled me. No matter how hard things get or how beat-up I get, I will survive. Just like that emblem. I had lost four of my favorite people in my life, yet I knew somehow I would survive. That Toyota emblem is still with me today, although it's no longer hanging on my wall.

I believe I was at my least favorite corner on the planet four times with my truck before I felt like I had picked up most of the pieces. The days that I didn't take gloves, I ended up cutting my fingers and scratching my arms, but that was all part of it. I knew it needed to be done, and I felt like it had to be me. The roses on the light post that were once fresh and living became wilted and lifeless, while the glow sticks that were taped to the post lost their shine. I felt like it was a place for me to go from death to life. The first time I was there, I couldn't possibly see how I was going to get through this. By the time snow was flying in the fall, I felt like it was a place for me to go where I felt alive and at peace. There was always something there; some sign. Something that made me smile and feel good inside. Whether it was birds singing in the cat tails or a light, cool rain, or maybe even a slow, soft snowfall—there was always a reason to smile. I always made a choice to see the good.

FAMILY IS EVERYTHING. WE HAVE GROWN

DESPITE THE CHALLENGES we faced as a family, I firmly believe that what happened just after New Year's 2016 has made us very resilient people in our own right. Not only am I proud of Mom and Tana, but also of myself. We have all come a very long way, and we have more to go, I'm sure.

Our family conversations and get-togethers are now far, far different—no doubt. There is always a feeling of a few empty chairs around the table, and always a missing smile or two. Those four are forever on our minds, and more often than not in a really great way. Or at least, that's how I feel and how I see the room when we are together as a family.

Still, there are often tears when we least expect it from one or more or us. I am sure that will always be the case. Often we don't even talk about it. We all just share a quiet understanding that a thought or some words triggered a memory or a sadness of sorts. We get each other in a way like we never did before. We are closer mentally, emotionally, and spiritually.

As the days, weeks, months, and years pass by, I know that our four angels will always have a profound impact on us. I also know that the hurt will never truly go away. Rather, we will learn how to accept it, acknowledge it, and figure out a way to navigate through it. There simply is no way of going around the pain, and we can never know when thoughts or feelings will pop up, often at the most inconvenient times.

Together we stand, and here we are!! Sharing our true selves to help others as best we can as a family united in strength. I am so very proud, and I know Chanda, as my biggest cheerleader, is still doing just that! Her big smile and unfathomable strength is in us all, as is Jordan's deep caring and sense of humor, forever helping us with inner blessings. The two little ones fill us with fun-loving, carefree determination to make a difference in this world.

To no end, I am overflowing with love. I feel as though the worst thing that could possibly happen in my life has forced me to find who I really am. Perhaps for others as well.

NEVER FORGOTTEN

TO THIS DAY I still wonder about some of the people who were just as close to Chanda and Jordan as I was. Being married twice and divorced twice, I often consider how the two women I was once married to are doing. After all, they were at one time a big part of our family too.

Angela is my kiddos' mom, and I of course wonder how she coped and is coping. Although we split up 10 years ago, she was definitely part of Chanda's inner circle. I must say, Angela was and still is the glue in our boys' lives, without a doubt. And in 2016, when my mind was completely gone, I relied on Angela more than ever.

For the first year, when I was checked out of life, Angela kept me in line with everything related to our kids. I remember asking her to please let me know about absolutely everything that our boys were doing; school activities, sports, concerts, birthdays, when they were to come to my house or go to hers, and ALL other things. I would forget so much and had to ask her for weekly or sometimes daily reminders of what I needed to do or where I needed to be.

Inevitably, I still missed things sometimes, like hockey practices or picking up one of my boys from school. Once I was supposed to pick them up and I completely forgot. When I realized what I had done, I was so lost. I found myself sobbing in my car, thinking I was a terrible, terrible person. How could I possibly forget to pick up my own kids from school? Thankfully, those harsh hours or days weren't many.

There are no words to convey just how grateful I am to Angela for being the world's best mom when at times I felt like the world's worst dad. Raising kids in two homes is not easy, yet we seem to have done a fairly good job of it. I am also certain that I owe Angela a huge amount of credit for keeping us all on track during my most difficult days! I am truly grateful for her unwavering love for our boys, which I know spilled over to me somewhat during that time.

My second wife Melanie was the auntie whom Miguire and Kamryn loved dearly, just as much as anyone else in our family. Auntie Watermelon was the name Kamryn coined for Melanie, and right to the last day, that's what she was known as. Melanie's kind and caring heart had a special place with Chanda, Jordan, and the kids, and she was super close to them all.

I am forever grateful to Mel. We shared our grief over the loss of our four favorite people with one another closely and openly. I was more than thankful to have support from as many people as possible. Mel knew the two little ones just as well as I did, if not better. As a kind and nurturing person through and through, Kamryn and Miguire were naturally drawn to her.

There is some disconnect in how tragedies like our families' are dealt with by Victim Services. Some people can easily be forgotten about or perhaps left out in the cold, and I believe Mel definitely fit into this category. I spoke to my Victim Services person Tracy about some of the folks that didn't have access to the help or resources that the rest of us did. Mel was my ex-wife, therefore Victim Services didn't reach out to her. I voiced my opinion and made sure that would happen, and eventually it did. Perhaps in future, this is something that won't be missed, as it's important to help everyone who is involved in a tragedy.

I owe many thanks to both Melanie and Angela for everything they did during those terribly hard days when I felt so lost and broken. At times, Mel and I would message back and forth, helping each other through our grief process. We had many conversations about the kids and some of the great memories we shared, and we exchanged pictures of the kids. On occasion, the same happened with Angela.

It also became very apparent that our support system reached far and wide. We received messages from people all over the world, including some we didn't even know. Virtual hugs and heartfelt messages were the norm. Counselors, coaches, and anyone with grief training of any kind were reaching out to us. To this day, I am still amazed at the outpouring of kindness we had from so many wonderful people.

Relying on my exes like I did may seem weird to some, however, I needed all the help I could get. In a strange way, it brought me closer to them both in a different way than before. There was love between us, or at least, that's what I felt and expressed. I can still love the woman who birthed my children and helped me navigate my toughest days even though we have been split for six years plus. I can still share some love with a woman who knew my niece and nephew—our niece and nephew—just as well as I did.

I was different, they were different, we were all very different. Our hearts were open and we shared, and we still do. I am grateful for it all. I couldn't have made the leaps and strides I did without them. I couldn't have been on point or at least more on point with my kids if their momma wasn't so kind as to keep me up-to-date with their activities.

SAGE AND HUDSON

MY TWO BOYS learned of their cousins', auntie's, and uncle's horrific fate while on holidays in Mexico with their mom. In conversation with them later, I asked them about their recollections.

They told me that they enjoyed the time away from our sometimes harsh winter with their mom. With the ocean breeze blowing, waves crashing in, and endless food and drink, the resort they were staying at was paradise for two boys of nine and eleven years old. Apparently Sage overate so much at the all-inclusive resort that he threw up in the ocean once! Full of laughter and life, they giggled as they told me about the red floaters in the ocean. It was an easy way to break into a conversation about what happened.

They recounted that Angela took the news very hard. She sat on the terrible news for a couple of days before she sat her two kids down on the balcony of the suite where they were staying. The boys shared that she began very sheepishly with, "There was a terrible accident, and Auntie Chanda, Uncle Jordan, Kamryn, and Miguire were all killed by a drunk driver." She was calm and quiet as she delivered the harsh news.

They told me that their mom's voice started cracking and became increasingly sad as she spoke, overcome by emotion and tears as she conveyed to our boys that a large part of the Mierau family was gone forever.

Being halfway through their holiday at that time, it felt somber to be in Mexico, not knowing for sure exactly what was happening back in Canada for the last few days of beach and delicious food. They didn't know what would happen when they got home, how other people were doing, or when the funeral would be.

After landing back in Saskatoon, the boys and their mom met up with me at the hotel where I was staying. We hadn't seen each other for about 10 days. We cried and hugged, happy to see one another again and aware that there was now a large hole in our lives.

Hudson recalled staying at the Holiday Inn with me that night, as the funeral was the very next day. We all shared our thoughts and memories about the funeral. Hudson remembered the small bus we took to go to the cemetery before we lowered the urn into the ground.

Sage talked about coming home from Mexico with whooping cough (the real reason for the red floaters in the ocean). He was still coughing in dramatic fashion at the funeral, and he even vomited during the luncheon after spinning and running around with Uncle James. We all chuckled as we remembered this brief bit of laughter during a not-so-fun time.

Our discussion led to how different family members were and are doing. Hudson said that I had been "in a down slump," but not doing too bad—at least initially. They both said that now, after some time has passed, I was doing "so much better with it than some of the others are."

"Mom (Angela) is doing ok," they told me. "At first she was sad for a while, but it wasn't too long and she was doing good." They both agreed that she occasionally talked about their cousins and auntie and uncle being gone, but she seemed to be doing good overall.

When we started to talk about Grandma Marie, we all agreed that she was still having a hard time. They said, "Grandma seems sad. Perhaps different in a way. Will Grandma be ok?"

Sage and Hudson talked about how Miguire wanted to play mini sticks the last time we saw them, just days before the accident. They spoke of

Kamryn's never-ending energy to play games with anyone and everyone when she got to see them.

It was a great conversion with two amazing young men who, in my opinion, are doing extraordinarily well considering the things they have endured. They seem smart for their years and full of sharp insights about how they see others navigating through sorrow, grief, and anger. I could not help but be extremely proud of who they had become.

Our candid conversation ended with laughter and an agreement that we were all doing ok, and that being ok was ok. As Sage recapped, "It's ok to think about this in a different way and find something good to come out of it. Even though others may not be there yet or maybe will not ever be."

I was filled with joy after our half-hour conversation about how life had been for the last four years, knowing that they were doing well, or even better than I had thought they were. It sort of hit me that gathering thoughts from others around me in order to share everyone's stories had helped me have some conversations I possibly may not have had otherwise; the conversation with my own kids being one of them.

Turns out I have even more reason to be thankful. Not just for how great my sons are, but also for how great our support system has been. I am intensely grateful to their momma Angela and her parents Bob and Doreen! It would have been near impossible to manage without such wonderful people in Sage and Hudson's support team. They say it takes a village to raise kids, and I can attest to that without question.

Although we had chatted briefly about all of this over the course of the previous four years, this was really the first time we went over it all. Before, they did not seem to want to open up about it much, or perhaps they felt I didn't want to. Either way, I was incredibly happy with our chat. I got the sense that they were more open about it because it was for my book, which was completely ok.

Now nearing 17 and 15 years old, my two young men gave me a quick rundown of what their next school day looked like as we adjourned from our discussion. I was left feeling satisfied that all was well, and they left giggling about something pertaining to the next day's events at school. Life is good.

I WILL NEVER FORGET THE DAY I HEARD THE NEWS

ANGIE, MY SWEETHEART, confidant, and the most amazing woman on the planet, came into my life in 2016. She knew both of my sisters, as they had both been directly involved in her business as Mary Kay consultants. When the news came out about a family of four hit by a drunk driver, Angie had a gut feeling that someone she knew had been involved in the incident. This chapter is in her own words and writing as she recalls how events unfolded for her. Written in January 2020, it also includes her take on some of the things that transpired between 2016 and 2020.

"Family of 4 killed by a drunk driver at the end of Wanuskewin road." I was in Hawaii when I saw the headlines on Facebook, and I INSTANTLY knew that it was going to turn out to be someone I knew. I searched and searched for more details for the rest of the day, without finding any answers. I went to bed feeling sick. When I woke at 5 am the next morning, I instantly remembered the accident and again opened my phone to search for names. Within the hour, I had found it. The Van De Vorst family—CHANDA! I couldn't believe it. Chanda was one of my Mary Kay team members, and her sister Tana was a really good friend of mine! I was the MC at Tana's wedding, the only person in attendance who was not family, and we sat with Chanda and her family at supper. Without wasting a second, I texted Tana, hoping it wasn't true. No answer. I called—again, no answer, just her voicemail. I left a message, knowing that if this indeed was true, she would need support—and tons of it.

As I lay there in bed thinking, letting it sink in, I could not stop the tears. How could this be?! I wished and prayed that somehow the names were wrong. I hoped that Tana would call back and tell me it wasn't true. I got up, went outside, and stood at the shoreline looking out at the ocean. How could the God that created this world of beauty allow something so horrible to happen? I wondered. I cried for a long time but still had some hope that it was just a mistake. I heard someone stirring back at the condo and noticed my sister out on her deck. I walked over and told her the news, and she just sat there, her eyes big and her mouth open. She had no words.

Tana later responded to my message, telling me that I had not heard wrong. I promised I would be there for the funeral and made arrangements to leave paradise a day early. I was filled with aching. How could this happen? How could this beautiful family be gone? I remembered them—the way they loved, yes not just lived but loved each day to the fullest. I remember thinking every time I saw them how they truly LIVED each day together with joy. I remembered that I admired how great they were at capturing any and all moments on camera. I loved looking through the posts Chanda made on Facebook; seeing the kids growing. I remembered how much I admired Chanda and how whenever I saw her she had a huge smile on her face, 100% of the time. She was one of those people; you know, the ones that make you want to be with them because their aura of positivity, kindness, and love just radiates and draws you in. This just seemed wrong. It couldn't be real!

The day of the funeral, our MK (Mary Kay) girls gathered and sat together for the service. I went a little early to drop off some MK items for the display of memorabilia. The church was huge, and it was packed. Hundreds gathered to honor the beautiful family. There was so much love, but just as much pain. The memorabilia display showed beautiful memories and symbols of what they all loved most. It was a beautiful service. I watched Tana from behind. Her slumped shoulders, her many tears. I also looked for Chanda's father-in-law. He and I had worked together for many years. He must have been devastated, losing his son and family. Tana blew me away by being able to sing to close the service. She pulled it off with strength and grace. I admired her strength, courage, and love for her sister to be able to put emotion aside and sing like that.

Hundreds and hundreds of people gathered for lunch after the service. With my family still out of the country, I was in no hurry. I gave Tana a quick hug and told her to tend to the others she needed to see, and that we would be waiting when she was ready. Ninety minutes or more later, she made her way back to us. She hugged me, exhausted pain written all over her. She looked drained and grief-stricken. We formed a circle of support around her. After a few minutes of talking, I noticed her brother Chad walking towards us. I had met him the year before at Tana's wedding and enjoyed the conversation we had. His questions about our business were sharp, and I admired his business mind. I remember thinking I was grateful that both Tana and Chanda had a business influence like him in their lives, as it would be an asset when they really wanted to start building their MK businesses.

As he walked towards me, I could feel his energy. It emanated pain! I walked towards him and embraced him as I told him how sorry I was for his loss. I knew that he and Chanda were VERY close. She always talked about him with admiration and love. I could feel the brokenness in him. I had never before been able to feel so strongly the feelings of someone I had only met once. He seemed to need the embrace and held me tight. When he let go and looked at me with painful tears in his eyes, I noticed how blue they were—just like his sisters'. We all stood in this circle and talked about many things—the accident, the week of events since, the feelings, how everyone was doing. At one point in the conversation, the subject of Tana's teaching job came up. My head did a turnabout when I heard the next words come out of Chad's mouth: "With all that has gone on, with the example of how short life can be, when are you going to start doing what you want instead of everything everyone around you expects of you?"

Wow—this guy had balls! Tana laughed and replied, "Point taken!"

Fast forward some time...I had been to see a medium, and almost my entire reading had been about Chanda and the kids. The "brother/uncle" was mentioned dozens of times! Over and over, Chad came up in the reading. I had actually planned to cancel the appointment, and I offered it to Tana, but she told me she wasn't ready for an appointment like that. She admitted she was hoping I would go because she was sure the answers she wanted would be revealed to me and I would be able to tell her after. I set a time to tell her what I had learned, and I revealed the things I thought she could handle. It went ok, but my poor friend was still in such depths of pain.

After that I had this deep calling to message Chad. It kept coming back, over and over, so I was obedient to the call. I wasn't sure how he would react. Not all people are open to this type of thing, but I knew I had to try. The feeling in me was too strong to ignore. He messaged me back shortly after, and he gave me his number. I called and the conversation flowed very easily. He was so open to anything I told him. He cried at some points but overall was so grateful and seemed to receive some level of comfort from the message I delivered; at least, that's what it felt like to me! This was all at a time in my life when turmoil was in full throttle. I was in the process of getting divorced, and it was ugly, unpredictable, and painful. I think helping Tana and her brother was a way to keep me feeling like I was doing good somewhere.

Time passed. Life had changed for me, and Chad and I started having conversations. I loved talking to him. I found it amazing how he understood so much of what I was going through and had been through over the years. He listened with full attention and let me talk about everything that was on my mind. Even though I was bitter and angry due to the turmoil in my life, I never felt judged, no matter what I said.

I loved the way his mind worked and the way he thought about things. I loved that he was so willing to be open and vulnerable and didn't hide or dismiss his feelings. He was open about the level of grief he was feeling, and I admired that. I had told myself when my marriage ended that I was going to stay single for years, until my kids left home. How could this happen now? This was supposed to happen years down the road! We both had children! We lived in different communities and both had very full work commitments. We both had our share of baggage. How could this be something that was supposed to be happening now?!

As poor as the timing seemed to be, the connection was so good! Chad could read how I was doing in the first 10 seconds of a phone conversation, and I could do the same for him. He had some really bad days then, as they were dealing with the aftermath of a family wiped out and all that brings. Some days when we talked he was good, and some days he struggled. Through it all though, I was impressed by his ability to get through it. He kept a good attitude most of the time, but there were days he would just break. I felt really helpless at those times because we were at the point where we were just talking. Had we been in a place where this wasn't so new, I may have been able to help out in more practical ways, but we just weren't there yet.

He had a road repair business at the time, and the work season was in full swing. From what he told me, he and the crew used to put in long days—12- to 16-hour days—almost every day. That year that wasn't happening as much, due to weather stopping progress. As business-minded and driven as he was, I could see that his fire was dim. Many days it seemed that he went through the motions, and from what he told me, he was laser focused the years before that. Some days it seemed as though getting through the day was as much as he could muster. It wasn't like he was overcome with sadness and emotion, but more like he was numb and just putting one foot in front of the other, taking care of one task at a time.

Through all of this, he was really good at being there for me, and I think he sometimes liked to take a break from his own thoughts by hearing about what was going on with me. It was a painful time, and

I too was getting through the ups and downs of raising children with someone who was no longer my spouse and all that brings. Chad was my light in all of this. Sometimes I wondered if he seemed so great because things were so scary, sad, and hard. Or was he really that good? After months of phone conversations, we started "dating", and all my wondering was laid to rest! In no time I had completely fallen in love with him like I never knew possible. I just loved who he was and the way he dealt with the heart of the situation. He didn't hold back from painful conversations. He was actively grieving and working his way through it all, and I admired his courage and strength. He wanted to be better and to find a way to believe this loss was not all for nothing. Chad was never outwardly angry with Catherine. He was sad and grieving yes, but he always said that there had to be more. He loved Chanda so deeply, and he missed her so much. She was his best friend, and he would sometimes break down, longing to hear her voice and reassuring words. He missed the kids, especially his little buddy Miguire. I remember watching them at Tana's wedding when Miguire was a little over a year old and he was absolutely shadowing his uncle. Wherever Chad was, Miguire was not far behind. I remember noticing what a special uncle/nephew relationship they had. Even when Tana and I were going through her wedding photos, it seemed that Miguire and Chad were always together. He missed them all every day, but he just seemed to know that there was more to it. He seemed to need to make sense of how the loss was going to make a positive difference to people. He wasn't sure who, when, or where—he just knew it would.

There were a couple of days when he broke down in a different way. Kamryn had donated some of her precious organs, and every once in a while, the family would get update letters from the recipients. When they would get the news that the recipients were doing well and learn how these children's lives had completely changed, Chad would smile through his tears. It was so sad yet so happy all at once. It was a reminder that his niece was gone, yes, but that she had been able to make such a difference for so many with her premature death. Those letters seemed to come when they were needed most.

I didn't really know Chad before the accident, so to tell you how he is different now would be a guessing game for me. I have wondered and have asked both Tana and his mom. They said he is a little softer now and lives more in the moment. I know that I see a real change in his spirit close to holidays, especially Christmas. He is usually very positive and optimistic, however, when the holidays are approaching, that positivity slips somewhat. He has told me on more than one occasion that since his dad passed, Christmas has not been the same, and of course without little ones, Christmas doesn't have the same excitement. I believe that it is hard for him for those reasons, yes, but also because Christmas was the last time he saw his sister, brother-in-law, niece, and nephew alive. They had a great time together and made such great memories, with no idea that those would be the last memories they made. To him, Christmas is a reminder of loss. It reminds him how much he misses his best friend and that this is never going away. There will always be four chairs that are empty FAR before they should have been.

I personally feel so grateful that I knew Chanda, Jordan, and the kids. I think me knowing how truly special they were is of comfort to Chad. I too have had sudden loss through accident in my life, and although it was not the same, it helps me to understand what he is feeling. Had the accident not happened, would Chad and I be together? Probably not! It's ironic how such tragedy can change the trajectory of your life and result in paths crossing with someone you would never have expected to know. He is the love of my life. I have never met someone that I admire, respect, and truly love to be with. I have never felt so heard and understood. There is nobody like my Chad—his heart is huge, and he is sentimental and loving. He is strong and driven. He takes risks and truly follows the path he feels he is led to. He is wise and courageous and the greatest gift. I never imagined someone would come into my life who could fill my heart like he does. At times I feel a little guilty knowing that tragedy struck and through it I found my soulmate and a love I never knew was even possible. But I know that it would make Chanda smile that great big smile of hers.

MOMMA MIERAU

IN THE SPRING of 2020, I wanted to have a more in-depth conversation with my mom to get a better feel for how she was doing and also to allow her an opportunity to share her thoughts and feelings about everything. After all, it was and always has been my intention to have all my family as well as Catherine's share whatever they would like to contribute to my book. I would have loved to have our conversation in person, however it happened to work out that it was a phone call. Before this conversation, our talks about what happened in early 2016 were mostly just bits and pieces, and I believe that it just took a considerable amount of time before one or both of us were ready to really talk about it. I have notated nearly the entire conversation to the best of my recollection.

"What do you remember about the day you learned about the accident?" I asked Mom. "Where were you? Who phoned you, and how did that all go?"

"Well, I was at home, and I think it was at four in the morning. Some RCMP officers or whoever, I don't even know if they were local guys or who, were at my door and they asked to speak to me and come into the house," Mom replied matter-of-factly. "I said I guess so. What else was I going to say?" She said she was scared and cautious. Then the officers told her that there had been a collision, but they didn't really elaborate any further.

"I don't even know if they told me that Jordan and Chanda had already passed on the scene; I can't remember that part. But anyway, they said to me, do you have any questions?"

I took in the words mom was sharing with me, and I couldn't help but wonder if her mind had been in a fog like mine was on that terrible night. It had to have been.

"I said well, not right now," Mom continued. "I don't know what happened, so I don't know if I have questions." Then the officers asked her if she would be interested in going to the city, and she said yes. She also thought that she had phoned me at that point.

Mom explained that the officers went over to Doug's, her neighbor across the street and our great family friend. "They asked if he would take me in," Mom recalled. "So that was fine, because Doug's wife Annette was already in the hospital." Mom was unsure whether that was based on my suggestion to the officers or if they had thought of it.

"What did you feel when officers showed up at your door talking about some kind of a collision?" I asked Mom.

"I can't say that I really felt anything because they didn't really elaborate on what had happened, so it only really struck me when I got to the hospital and everybody was there."

"So you went all the way to Saskatoon not really knowing anything at all other than that there was a collision basically?" I asked sheepishly.

"Yes," she replied quickly. She shared that she called me just before leaving the house to see if I knew anything more about Miguire, but I didn't phone back. "I think the officers had something to do with that. I'm not sure, but that was my thought at that time. So I didn't really know anything, and the trip into the city was pretty quiet because what are you supposed to think?" Mom said. "Doug said to me, 'are you ok?' Well, how do you answer such a question? Hard to know if you're ok when you don't know exactly what happened. Things kind of just clicked when I got to the hospital," she continued. I was a bit taken back to hear her convey that she did not know Chanda and Jordan were gone already before she even left her house.

"When you got to the hospital, who was already there?" I asked my momma to see if she remembered it the same as I did. There was no doubt that we were helping each other fill in some blanks where our memories of that day were less than perfect.

"Well you, Mel, Linda and Lou, and Lou's brother were already there. Or was it just Linda and Lou?" Mom answered. "That's where my memory fails me. I don't remember the first family being there," she recalled. We agreed that Jordan's mom and dad, Linda and Lou, were there first.

"Everybody was in Kamryn's room, and you had Miguire in your arms because he had already passed," Mom recalled with obvious emotion in her voice. I was in complete awe listening to her recount what she saw when she arrived at the hospital, as I really was unaware of the timeline as to who arrived and when. Mom helped me fill in some of the holes in my memory. "Yeah, we took turns holding Miguire right in Kamryn's room, and I can't remember if Lou's brother was there or not. I know he was there at some point, but if he was there right away, I don't know that."

Mom continued, "I mean, as the day went on people would gather, more people would be there. I forget what time Tana and James got there. It was quite a while later."

"What do you remember about Kamryn's diagnosis or what they told you when you got there?" I enquired.

"Well, she was definitely on a lot of machines and everything, and she was covered up. You could only see her face," Mom responded.

"Were you actually there when they tested her to see if she was brain-dead?" I asked apprehensively. "I can't remember. They did it twice, and I was at her side both times. I don't think there were any other people in the room." In previous conversations, Mel had shared with me that she too was in the room during these tests. "I know Jordan's family didn't want to see that," I said.

"Ok, let's put it this way, you guys might have been in the room, but we were outside right close by," Mom reminded me. "Linda and Lou were outside. I was there, Tana and James, Shirley was there, Andrea was there, and Kennedy as well. It then became time to make a quick decision. We were all in the room with her on the bed; all the family members that were there. It was literally a two-minute conversation. It was very quick, and we were all very clear about what we wanted to do. We all said yes immediately with very little discussion," Mom shared, overwhelmed with emotion yet with a strong sense of gratitude. "You know our family had the opportunity to help somebody else in need." Mom was referring to the organ donation decision.

When I asked Mom more about it, as I was trying to really have her share more about how she was feeling at that time, she responded, "I think I just accepted the fact that her body could not go on any longer, and if somebody can keep on living with whatever we could give away from her, I thought that would be great. I really didn't put much thought into it because at that time we just thought it was the right thing to do. I think it was just like, ok this is the last time I'm going to see her and it's our goodbye. I remember going in and out a couple of times just to touch her and give her a kiss." Mom swallowed a lump in her throat with obvious emotion.

"I don't remember the room full of doctors and nurses," I said. "I don't know how many exactly, but to me it seems like there were five or six people in the room to do the test; I'm not sure if I remember," I said.

Mom replied, "I think we just kind of put one foot in front of the other because when the doctors or nurses told us to do something, that's what we would do."

I then asked Mom what she remembered about the family room when the officer came to talk to us to tell us what had happened and what he saw.

"He told us what he tried to do with Miguire to save him," she answered. "It was also a very emotional time for him because he had children, and he wondered what this would do to everybody else's lives. And yeah, it was very upsetting for him. I remember that. He said he tried very hard to keep him going until he could at least get to the hospital."

Mom and I both agreed that's what we heard him tell us all.

"The officer shared with us that it was a T-bone," I said. "I remember him saying that the driver was out of her jeep and she was wandering around looking for her cell phone, and that she was thinking that she had been hit."

Mom cut in, "She was lost and thought she was on the other side of the city!"

I then asked the hard question. "What do you remember about going to see Chanda and Jordan in the basement of the hospital?"

"Well, Jordan certainly didn't look like himself, and Chanda's arm was up like that because she had injuries inside her neck," Mom said. "I think I gave her a hug, I'm not sure. I think I said goodbye baby girl."

It was so hard to hear the shaky voice of my own mom saying the words, "goodbye baby girl."

"The room was cold and bodies were cold," she continued. "They even still had their winter jackets on."

"Anything else from the hospital that comes to mind?" I asked.

"I remember food being brought in," she responded. This was an interesting fact for me to learn, as I had zero recollection of any such thing happening. We discussed that it was friends of Jordan's family that had brought in food for us all. Strange how my mind had completely forgotten that part altogether.

"Do you remember the cast forms of the feet and the hands they made?" Mom asked.

"Yes, I do," I said."

"They brought that to the family room so we could see them, and I've never seen anything done like that before. I was very, very amazed," Mom shared with excitement. "And we got to take home the blanket that Kamryn was covered in."

"Where is that now?" I asked.

"I've got it in my house," she said.

Mom and I conversed for a few minutes about who stayed where for the week in-between the day of the incident and the funeral. Her memory was better than mine about this as well. The amazing support that came pouring in came in many forms. A few hotels offered free rooms to our family, which we used for a couple of nights before the funeral. We both recounted how grateful we were for people's generosity.

In previous conversations, my boys told me that they got home from Mexico with their mom on Friday and the funeral was on Saturday; we didn't go home before it. They stayed with me in the hotel. I sort of remember that Friday night when they got home and stayed with me, but I do not remember where I stayed the rest of the week.

"What do you recall about the contents of the house and putting the house up for sale?" I then asked Mom.

"Well, Linda and Lou had gone through everything before we had a chance to do that. They just told us, this is your box for you and you go through it and this is a box for you and that's how it was, but not the kitchen stuff," she recalled. We talked briefly about some of the kitchen contents that I happen to have a lot of in my home. "Most of the toys went to the food bank I think, because they used them as gifts for kids. And all the kids' clothes went to schools."

"We eventually did get a key, and we went to the house and got the photographs that were hanging on the walls?" I asked Mom, as my memory was lacking on this front as well. I loved all of the photos Jordan had made into bigger prints to hang on the walls. Now they are in my home and always will be.

"Jordan's family got one of their friends to paint the house before we listed it for sale," Mom said. "I mean, for me the house is just a house, it wasn't really a big thing for me when it was all cleaned out and listed, saying my last goodbyes…you know, to the house. The place we used to go to visit was more significant for me than the materialistic item of the house." Mom only went by the house once more a few months after it was sold.

I responded, "For the first couple of years I probably went by the house maybe every three or four months, and now I still go by it once a year, more so to see how the oak tree in the front yard that Jordan planted is doing than anything else."

"I want to get back to the school sometime and see the bench," Mom shared. We lovingly recounted our experience at Kamryn's kindergarten, where they had a buddy bench on the playground with Kamryn's name on it in honor of her. More than once I have found myself sitting on the Kamryn buddy bench during the day when all the kids were in school.

Getting back on topic, I said, "I didn't really feel the need to have anything out of the house other than what I gave the kids for Christmas. I thought it was a cool memory to have the hockey sticks and Barbie doll I had given them. Nothing else really has much significance for me. However, if I'm in my kitchen making something and I use the pepper and salt shaker that came from their house, I do remember that a little bit."

Mom and I talked about the time between the hospital saying goodbyes and the day of the funeral. It's crazy how the human mind forgets things in times of stress and grief. We shared our best recollections of when we went to the graveyard and Remco to look at examples of headstones. We agreed that their headstone is incredibly beautiful and "extravagant", in Mom's words.

Mom recounted that John from the funeral home had made everything very comical. He didn't want it to be a sad affair. I agreed, remembering how amazing John had been at making us all feel as good as possible during such a tough time.

To our best ability and recollection, we discussed the day of the funeral and what it was like at the grave site. Mom recalled, "We went out to the grave site and we threw some things in the ground along with their ashes." I too remembered this, as I had been more than honored to lower one of Miguire's mini sticks into the hole, as if to tell him I was thinking about him playing hockey up in heaven amongst the stars.

It was frigidly cold the day of the funeral, so we took a bus there. Mom reminded me that we were all given something to place in the hole. I had to really push my memory to bring back some of these things I had forgotten.

"We all put some dirt in the hole, is that what you're thinking?" I asked hesitantly. "Or was it something else? I can't remember that part." Neither Mom nor I really remembered for sure just exactly how that went.

"It's funny, every time I have this conversation it's not as though I remember more, it's just making me think about it a little deeper to see if I can bring up more details," I told Mom. "Anything else from the funeral that comes to mind?" I asked. "My recollection is that the church was crazy full with 1200 people; it was amazing."

We had food and visited with all our family and friends that were there to celebrate four amazing people. It is a wonderful memory; to think that nearly every single family member from both the Mierau family (my dad's family) and the Bartel family (Mom's family) were there. After lunch and a few hours of visiting, we had the most amazing experience as a family. We had many, many glow sticks to put in the snow banks outside the church in memory of our four angels. It is such a great memory for us all.

Mom and I then chatted about what life had been like after all the things with the estate and belongings had been taken care of, and I asked her, "So what did the remainder of 2016 look like for you after the house was sold and everything we needed to do was sort of done?" I don't know if I could have prepared for what she said next. It made my heart hurt and my eyes leak.

She hesitated and then answered, "Well, I'm going to back up to before the house was sold. I remember the first family day holiday. I was here all by myself and it was a tough day. I don't know where everybody else was." Her voice cracked with obvious emotion. "I don't know if I've ever cried like that before, but I did" she sobbed.

Oh shit, I thought to myself. Where was I that day? Why wasn't I with mom? Disappointed in myself, I was lost in thought for a brief moment while Mom kept sharing. I was beating myself up inside!

I recomposed myself and sheepishly shared, "Yeah, I had days like that too. Some days where I didn't even get out of bed. I'd just get up to pee and have a shot of water once in a while, and I'd just cry." Mom was quiet; regrouping. We both needed a minute to get through the emotional memories that those days brought up for us.

As if to change the tone of the conversation, Mom firmly stated, "But after the house was sold, I still had lawyer stuff to do, so I was still doing paperwork and working through it all with Linda over phone calls and all that kind of stuff." Choking down the lump in my throat, I quickly chirped "Yes!" as if to assure her I was still listening, albeit from a more emotional place inside myself.

Mom then spoke about the time when we were at the crown prosecutor's office to talk about sentencing, how long we should go for, and what we all thought about it. Mom agreed with me that there were many differing opinions and emotions in those meetings. She shared, "That was predetermined all right. Of course we didn't like it, but there wasn't much we could do about it. Our belief in the justice system is broken."

"What are your thoughts about the penalty that she received?" I offered her another chance to share her thoughts about the legal end of things. I added, "The hard part was when we read our victim impact statements, if there is anything you want to share about that day or time."

"Well…I don't think anybody thought it was fair what she got at the time, but serving a sentence might not be an answer for all of that kind of stuff either, so it's tough to say. I mean, did she learn a lesson from the amount of time she got? We will probably never know that, will we?" she asked. "It was a very tough day in court, and I wanted to see her walk out with the shackles on and cuffs. I saw tears when she was reading what she had to say," Mom continued. "I wasn't quite sure if that was true either. I mean, at that time, what are you going to believe?" Mom had clearly wondered whether Catherine's words truly came from her heart and whether or not her tears had been fabricated. "And then we heard that she was going to the healing lodge. We thought that was pretty cushy then too," she reminded me.

I had forgotten that. "Did we hear about the healing lodge in court?" I asked.

"Yes, we did," Mom assured me. "But we didn't know at that time exactly when she would be going there."

Mom further remembered that we had gone out for tacos after court that day in a little cafe that Jordan had talked about. "They had good fish and chips. I don't remember the name of it, but it was good." I again realized that I apparently had zero memories of food during a lot of those hard days.

"That day in court when we read our victim impact statements was probably one of the hardest days of my life," I told Mom.

She replied, "I was literally exhausted that day. I don't think anybody understood a word I said. I didn't want to read mine because I didn't think I would be able to read it anyway, as there would be so many tears in my eyes…how much reading can you do?" she asked, as if to question the point of even doing it.

"Do you remember seeing Catherine's daughter?" I asked curiously. "She looked like her mother."

"Yeah, we kind of thought it might be her daughter. We saw those girls run out too, or was it just one? I forget," Mom said. "Yeah, we saw they were beautiful girls and they had dark hair, so we just presumed they must have been from Catherine's family."

I agreed with mom and proceeded to ask a question that I didn't remember ever asking before. "What are your feelings on the healing lodge?"

Mom said, "I guess it doesn't really matter, but why did they move her over? Will she learn a lesson or change some of the things that aren't right in her life? And does it matter whether she is in a healing lodge or in prison? Ultimately, it's the work you put into yourself to heal or figure out what the hell's going on in your life. You know, come out of incarceration as a better person and do the right things in life instead of the wrong things you are doing when you are sentenced, regardless of where you are at."

The words Mom said next were a bit of a surprise to me, to say the least. As if she was sharing a secret, she slowly said, "You know, I really have never ever thought about Catherine, I just haven't! It's not going to do me any good just to say to myself, well she shouldn't have done this, but in the end it did happen, so why even think about her and all that kind of stuff? So I kind of just put her out of my mind." She continued, "I haven't really ever thought about her because I guess the bottom line was it wasn't going to help me at all."

I, on the other hand, had thought about Catherine and her family almost right away after her sentencing. "Because her family is all messed up too," I told Mom. "It's not fair to her kids that she did what she did. It's not fair to anybody, so that's what got me thinking about her and ultimately what got me to write her a letter in August. You know, I'm sort of hanging on to the words that she said in court in her statement, and again this is my perception of it and perhaps it could be completely wrong compared to what other people may have heard, but I heard her say that she would spend the rest of her life trying to prevent this from happening to other families."

"Yes those are words, but she's also going to have actions," Mom rebutted.

To which I replied, "Yes, which is why I reached out to her in prison. I want to know where she is sitting with that. Has there been any action towards what she said? When I was running my marathon last year and learned that she was doing the same in prison and also raising money for MADD, I thought ok, well, that is a positive sign that she is doing something proactive towards prevention and getting the message out there and raising funds, and that's great!"

"I kind of wondered if she is ever confused about why or when or how come; all that kind of stuff. Or has she just kind of accepted that it happened. I wonder…" Mom shared with me.

"Yeah, I wonder that too," I replied.

"I think the first Christmas was very hard for all of us because we didn't know exactly what we should be doing; we were so lost," Mom said as we were discussing all the firsts. Birthdays, anniversaries, Thanksgiving, Family Day, Christmas, New Years, and the like.

"Empty chairs," I commented. That was the feeling we both had when all the firsts came and went. Empty chairs and empty hearts. "I think we all did our best at that time," I continued. "I know for me, after all the things were sort of looked after, like the funeral and house and contents, Christmas was the next hard thing. Their birthdays, like Miguire's birthday in September; I don't really remember the first one."

Mom reminded me, "We went to the beach and released balloons into the air and painted rocks."

As my memory was coming back I replied, "Yeah, I remember doing that, I just didn't know if it was the first one or the second one or which one we did, I just don't know."

Mom pondered and paused for a moment before saying, "Yeah, I don't remember which it was either. I think the first time we painted rocks…I think. But then again, who knows?"

We both agreed it had happened for sure and that it was likely on the first of Miguire's missed birthdays.

Christmas and New Year's seemed to always be the hardest for us. I hesitated and said, "I mean, I remember them at the bowling alley, I remember them at Christmas time; Miguire hitting the couch with this hockey stick and saying sorry to the couch in his super adorable two-year-old voice as if the couch had feelings and he perhaps had hurt them." I continued, "And New year's, you know, we go through the anniversary day and now that's different for everybody, but for me it's getting a little easier. I think this Christmas was better, although I don't really care for Christmas; I haven't since Dad died." Mom knew this. In my mind, Dad was the one with the true Christmas spirit, and without him around, it is just different.

"This year I think was better for me than the last three, so I see that as a good thing. But what are your thoughts? How do you feel about Christmas and New Year's and how they have been this past year and the years before since not having them around?" I asked Momma.

She searched for words for a moment. "Well, Chanda always made sure we were together at Christmas time, but we didn't ever really get together on New Year's Day." Mom and I both agreed that Chanda seemed to have been the glue that held us all together. She was the one who made plans for us all to come together as a family, no matter how busy everyone's schedules got.

"I think the first year we were just lost. So after that, as you say, I think it did get easier, and every year I light candles the day of the collision," Mom said with pride. I always admire her quiet strength when she talks about hard things like lighting candles in memory of her daughter, son-in-law and two grandkids who are no longer with her. Sometimes it stops me in my tracks to think about how hard it must be to lose a child...to lose one of my boys would be absolutely devastating. Is it different from losing a sister? Losing four loved ones at once? I try not to get stuck on those thoughts for too long, as I just don't want to think about it or imagine that scenario ever happening!

"I do light candles for their birthdays every year," Mom shared. I smiled and asked her if she still did glow sticks too. The day of the funeral with all our family and extended family there, we had many hundreds, if not thousands of glow sticks outside on the snow-covered ground, where we shaped them into hearts, the four's initials, or their names. It was a beautiful tribute we did, and it still fills me with love when I think about it. Even our home town held a vigil for the Van De Vorsts with glow sticks. I am forever grateful to the many people that shared in our pain and supported us in such an amazing way. When I asked Mom about glow sticks, it was because I was remembering those tributes we saw; thousands of people putting out glow sticks for a couple of weeks after the tragedy as well as on the anniversary day each year since. Mom and I had both put out glow sticks on the one-year anniversary of the accident, but neither of us have done it since.

After reminiscing about the glow sticks, I asked Mom if there was anything else that she wanted to share about 2016. She reiterated, "I know I tried to keep busy so I couldn't think of everything that happened in the past. I would do a lot of garden work; put it that way." Mom had always loved her gardens and took great pride in them. Occasionally I wondered if she was doing more gardening and working herself too much to keep her mind occupied with what she loves. Some years, she had four or five plots between her yard and her neighbors' yards. Often I reflect on what work or hobbies I do to get away or avoid things in my mind. It seems that we needed to do that for a while to let some of the pain subside in order to deal with it head-on at a later time.

My favorite gardener and I spoke of how our minds were in a grief fog for the entire year in 2016 and perhaps beyond, into other months or even years. Mom said that it was the same for her. "It didn't take much for my brain to wander either. I mean, you just out of the blue would think of something and off it would go. I don't think I accomplished a whole lot."

"How did you find your emotions in 2016?" I asked. "I could be anywhere, and at the drop of a hat I would just have tears and emotion. I would have no idea why it was triggered."

Mom replied with some emotion in her voice, "I was the same way, but then people would say to me that they didn't want me to cry. And that part always bugged me. And I figured, so I'm not supposed to show emotion? These were people that I worked with that would say that to me, and it bugged the heck out of me." I was a bit taken aback by her statement. How could people not have empathy and compassion for a woman who had lost a large portion of her family? What gives others the right to judge or the right to tell someone how they can or can't feel or grieve?!

"Sometimes you just want to avoid somebody because of the things they said in the past," Mom continued. I certainly can attest to this, as I too have had some people say or do things that I then just wanted to stay clear of for my own well-being.

The words that Mom said next stopped me dead in my tracks. Someone had actually said to her, "I don't understand why you are so upset. Your kids did not live here." What kind of a person would think that, let alone say it out loud to a person who is grieving?

"What did you say to that?" I asked.

"I didn't say anything, because what do you say? I turned around and walked away," she replied. I had a hard time wrapping my mind around that statement, and our conversation slowed down for quite some time.

After that we chatted about family for a few minutes, as I was curious about how her siblings had supported her. Her two sisters who live in the same community as she does are of course more supportive, as they see each other more often. Mom's other siblings are spread across western Canada with many miles between the 10 of them. Her closest sister Dorothy lives less than a block away, and they spend a great deal of time with one another and share a love of gardening. She sees Shirl, who also lives in town, less often, however she still provided some support to my Mom over the last few years in various different ways. Like with most families that live far apart, visits and phone calls seem to become fewer on both sides. I know this all too well. My siblings and I can go weeks or months without a phone call, or in my brother's case, years.

I then decided to dive a little deeper and asked, "If you were to say how you're doing now compared to four years ago when life was flipped upside down, how would you sum that up or what would you say?" I was not surprised when she replied, "I think I'm doing not too bad, like, I know I have to branch myself out in different directions now to make sure I don't stare at four walls all day long. I should say I have to find things to do or I have to do things, put it that way. I know I have lots of things to do, but you know, some days you just don't want to do them." I know this feeling all too well, as some days that's how I feel as well, although it's happening less often the more time passes. Mom continued, "I could say it's going better, yes absolutely, but there's always going to be a day where you just…yeah that kind of comes back to your mind."

I jumped in with my thoughts, "So you have a shit day once in a while!"

"Yup," Mom chirped.

"Do you think your mind or your memory are what they were before the accident, or is it still different?" I asked.

She said, "Oh boy, when you get to my age that's the multimillion dollar question."

"Well, even for me, I don't think I feel like I did in 2015 when I had the capability and capacity to run multiple businesses and really do well at it; and kids and life in general. And now I feel like I'm just not 100% back to that," I said.

Mom added, "I don't think I'll ever be, well, I guess I could say I feel like I dragged some days because I don't know what the reason is, but I don't know, it seems like you just don't want to do something, or that's why I say, when I do garden work I make sure I'm up early, and this time of the year (winter) I tend to stay in bed and mope around, which I shouldn't be doing. And so once the days get longer and brighter that makes a big difference."

"Yes, I would agree with that too," I replied. Then I confidently asked, "What do you think about me talking to Catherine's kids and sharing their perspective of all of this? I had conversations with them; I asked what kind of a family they have, what kind of a childhood they had; I went through all of that. What do you think of me doing that?"

Mom hesitated momentarily and then said, "Well I think it's very interesting just to see how the other side is doing or what they are going through. What they think of it all. And you know, they probably think of things differently than what we do because it's our family, but it is their mother that did it, so how do they perceive what their mother did? How do they think we should be coping? After talking to you, they probably have a good idea of what we have been through," Momma continued. "I give you a lot of credit for doing that, because I would never have the guts to do that; put it that way."

"That's what most people say," I responded.

She quickly added, "So, you might have to keep your back covered. I don't know what some people are going to do or say though."

"I don't really worry about that," I said. "I've been under the microscope for 10 years, with people judging me and saying whatever they feel like, so I don't really give a shit. They can have their opinions, good or bad, it doesn't matter to me." In the end, I fully believe that all of us openly sharing our story will help so many other people with different things in their lives, so it is all more than worth it! I just want understanding out of the whole thing. To be able to share everybody's story; here's how it's went for us, and here's how it went for you, and Tana, as well as Catherine's kids, and as many others as possible that this has affected. That way, when the reader picks up the book, they will really understand that this kind of thing doesn't just affect three people or four people or eight people or 10 or whatever their perception of it is. This affects multiple families and goes multiple layers deep!"

I continued, "Because we all know somebody who's struggling with grieving. We all know somebody who's struggling with alcoholism, who's lost their best friend; somebody who lost a daughter, somebody who lost a child—a loss of any kind, really. It's important to me that people have a better understanding from all different sides. How it's been, how we've been coping and how we are doing now. I think that it's valuable information that can be used by other people to help them in their lives."

"I would think losing four people at once would be very different from losing just one child," Mom replied. "I mean, you go through a lot of emotions and ups and downs regardless, but it's a very different scenario." As she said this, I realized that it wasn't really something I had considered too much. In reality, I suppose it is very different in every single way.

"For lack of better words, people can get stuck," I said.

Mom replied, "Well, I think yeah, some people are like that. They don't know how to move one step forward. I can't imagine some of these people that 20 years later, 30 years later still cannot get out of bed." We agreed that being open about our journey in order to shed light for others was super important.

"If you can help one person, you're doing something absolutely right!" I said.

We then talked about personal development and knowing that we needed to put some work in to be sure we were ok and or headed in the right direction after such a big loss. In February 2018, I attended a three-day course called 'The Basic', which was put on by PSI Seminars. Mom and Angie attended in the fall of 2018 and Tana in July of 2018. All three of them went to the advanced course called PSI 7 in San Francisco in February 2019. Mom and I agreed that it was super helpful to us all to have had the opportunity to take ourselves on in such a way. It helped us deal with grief and loss in a very positive and healthy way. I believe it has made me a far better communicator with people on a much deeper level, allowing me to have far more meaningful relationships with everyone in my life, including those I don't know well.

I attribute PSI Seminars to Mom's good mental health. We all noticed a very big difference in her immediately after she attended the courses. It has been a wonderful experience, one that we intend to keep building on as we pursue more personal development courses, counseling, and the like. In December 2019 I was able to have my kids, Sage and Hudson attend the Basic in Calgary as well, which was super exciting for me!! As Mom says about The Basic and PSI 7, "I learnt more about myself in those two courses than all the counseling I have ever done!"

We are all on this journey with a commitment to learn as much as possible about ourselves in order to heal, grow, and prosper, particularly through the hard times we have been through and are going through.

MY ELDEST SISTER TANA

I HAD AN IN-DEPTH chat with my sister Tana around the same time I had the conversation with my mother. Since Tana and I live about six hours away from each other, our conversation was also a call. One big difference between my call with Tana and the call with my mom was the fact that Tana and I had previously talked quite a few times about the crash and life since then. Our views on most of it had remained unchanged for the most part, although I am not so sure that Tana was as far along with forgiveness as I was. We had more frequent conversations mostly to figure out the best way to support Mom, which in turn helped us to support each other. In the spring of 2020, when I was deep into putting together this book of our families' story, I had great conversations with so many people. Both in my family and Catherine's, as well as with friends and strangers alike that connected with what I was sharing. I feel that it is pertinent that we share our families' story as in-depth and as widely as possible.

Tana answered the phone on the second ring, in anticipation of my call. She sounded excited. After a few minutes of conversation about the niceties of life such as work and weather, I asked her about the crash.

"Sister Tana, what do you remember about learning about the crash?" I asked. I was lying comfortably on my bed as I often do when I expect a long phone call with any of my family members.

"We were in Perdue. The phone rang at 5:30 am, and we ignored the call; as if anyone needs to be calling at such hour of the day, and back to sleep we went," Tana said. "Then, around 6:30 am, RCMP knocked on the door and James (Tana's husband) answered the door." Almost immediately, Tana knew something was terribly, terribly wrong.

"Tana, you better come now!" her husband shouted, his voice high-pitched and full of terror. She got dressed just enough to go to the door to see what was happening.

The officer spoke firmly and bluntly. "Ma'am, are you Chanda Van De Vorst's sister?"

Not knowing what to expect, Tana responded instantly with a lump in her throat, "Yes"!

"I am sorry to inform you that there has been an accident and Chanda and Jordan are dead," the officer said, not mincing his words. A few seconds or maybe a minute passed between that shocker of a statement and what was to come next. "Your nephew Miguire was also killed, and Kamryn is in ICU at RUH (Royal University Hospital)."

Of course Tana immediately asked, "How is Kamryn?"

The officer simply answered, "We don't know her condition, but it's critical, and we don't know how long she will stay alive."

The shock and devastation that set in for them both upon hearing the horrific news was instantaneous. "At this point, James was on the couch bawling, just not knowing what to do," Tana shared, her voice cracking. The officers left, as the worst part of their day was done. Tana went to the couch to take a second with James to attempt to gather their thoughts about the horrific news. What to do next? Within moments they knew that they needed to get to the hospital, and quickly.

In an attempt to hang on to some normalcy during the chaos, they cleaned up before rushing to the hospital. "We brushed our hair, brushed our teeth, and got dressed in decent clothes, almost as though we were leaving the house for a normal day. You're not though. It's an uncomfortable 45-minute drive to the hospital." While James was driving, Tana had to make the hardest phone call she may have ever made. "I had to call my boss to tell him I would not be in for work the following day." As a school teacher, she knew that giving her boss as much notice as possible was the best, although she was "almost certain he didn't understand what I was trying to tell him. Vocalizing what the officer told me was incredibly tough to say out loud over the phone."

Her recollection of when she learned it had been a drunk driver is a little foggy. My sister and I talked about Officer Matt telling us it was a drunk driver when we were all gathered in the family waiting room in the NICU at the hospital. She is almost certain she did not know until then, and I agreed that I did not know anything about the cause of the accident until Officer Matt told us what he saw as the first on scene. We spoke of what wording they used: "Accident, tragedy, or incident," Tana remembered. It's never really an accident when talking about drunk driving, where it is a choice to drink and then drive.

The whole concept of time eluded Tana during the time getting to the hospital. As they drove, many questions ran through her mind. "Where is Mom? Does she even know yet? Does Chad or Tyler know?"

Tana spoke of who arrived at the hospital when and how. "How did you get there before Mom, and Mom before me?" she asked. "I remember asking how to get into the pediatric unit, where was the damn phone to call them to open the door and let us in?" Once finally inside the ward where Kamryn and Miguire were, Tana had the sense that everyone was watching them as they walked down the hall all the way to the other end where Kamryn's room was. She wasn't sure whether people were actually watching them or whether that was just her perception at the time. "There were people sitting in Kamryn's room, or near it, or by the nurses' station, just crying!" she said. "You just don't think you will ever be in that kind of situation".

Tana knew for a fact that she and James arrived at 7:30 am. I asked, "When you got there, who all was there already?" as if to help jog my memory even further.

"You, Mel, Mom, Linda, Lou, and I do know Joel (Jordan's brother) and Chandra (Joel's wife) were not yet there, nor was Alyssa (Jordan's sister). I think Angie (Jordan's sister) was already there," Tana recalled. The next thing she said was something I did not remember or perhaps maybe never knew at all. "I know Joel and Chandra were not there yet, because that is why Miguire remained in his crib in his room so they could say their goodbyes as well." This brought tears to my eyes as I recalled very vividly holding Miguire for what seemed like many hours. I could still see the very clear image in my mind of him swaddled in the blanket, both in my arms and in the crib.

Tana also reminded me that we waited until everyone was there before we made our way downstairs to say our goodbyes to Chanda and Jordan. This was perhaps around late afternoon because their bodies were actually at a hospital across the city until we asked for them to be brought to us for viewing.

Tana brought my mind and attention back to the NICU when she said, "Once we were all there, we just spent the day consoling one another, spending time with Kamryn, spending time with Miguire, waiting for the doctors' decisions about brain damage and brain death." Tana's voice shook as she spoke. We shared a moment just remembering. Ah, it was so hard to hear my family reopen their wounds from that day. It took me right back to the emotion and devastation we all shared on that day.

"And of course, the focal point of the day was the transplant decision!" Tana said. "That two minutes—it was not long—was so powerful."

"Uh huh," I agreed. "It's funny that we all say two minutes; it was literally that or less."

"Yes, absolutely," Tana said. We talked about how amazing it was to have two families, with many in the room to discuss and decide whether or not to donate the organs of a loved one whom none of us were ever ready to say goodbye to. "It was amazing how we came to a unanimous decision so clearly, quickly, and decisively!" Tana said.

I then asked Tana about the test they did for brain function. "Were you in the room for the test?"

She responded quickly, "I was not in the room. I did not know it was an option to be in the room. I guess I assumed, and it was an assumption on my part that when they do those procedures nobody should be in the room…Now maybe that was my way of not being in the room because I couldn't handle it, or maybe I wasn't in the right place at the right time." I reminded her that I was in the room holding Kamryn's hand both times they did the test. I was completely oblivious to anyone else being there except Kamryn.

Tana then recalled, "I remember getting the results back and then going in the room."

"How did you feel when they gave us the results of that?"

She hesitated before answering, "I don't know if I know to be honest. Now this is gonna be a guess, but RELIEF. Together again as a family unit." I agreed with what she said next, "And I know if it were different we would have a totally different life at the moment, and we would be handling it just fine. When I walked in there, I knew it was going to be bad, so that maybe was the best result." We both agreed that the organ donation was the bright spot in an otherwise very, very dark time.

"I think the organ donation helped us out a little that day," I stated.

"I think it was much more than a little," Tana reaffirmed. "There is still hope that some good can come from it, and that other families are grateful. Perhaps that is a story still to come, that whenever they are ready we can meet them, but they have to be ready."

"I fully agree," I said. We were referring to the families that received Kamryn's organs. Perhaps one day we'd be fortunate enough to actually meet them.

Sister Tana Banana, as I used to call her in my younger years, recalled that we were asked a plethora of questions about Chanda, Jordan, and Kamryn, questions regarding their health and previous medical issues so that the hospital would know whether they would qualify for organ or tissue donation. Miguire, on the other hand, was not able to donate anything due to the length of time we held him and said our goodbyes; or at least, that is our recollection. Incredible detail went into the questions and answers we went through during the organ donation screening.

With obvious emotion in her voice, Tana said, "The decision to donate or not was not made by us. I believe Chanda or Jordan or both were there to make that decision for us. It was peaceful because it was made so unanimously."

I agreed, "There was nothing to decide."

"What do you remember about being in the family room and Officer Matt coming to tell us what happened?" I asked Tana.

"Just his compassion and how heavy his heart was," she said with obvious emotion in her voice. "AND bottom line was him holding Miguire's hand." I was right there with my sister as her voice shook. If there is one thing that really sticks in my mind and heart it's Officer Matt being there almost instantly and holding Miguire's tiny little hand. I am forever grateful that someone was there with my little man. "No 911 was needed, as he was there in moments," Tana reminded me. Officer Matt had shared with us that he happened to be patrolling on that stretch of road at the exact right time, and he was on scene before the dust even settled. She and I agreed that the rest of the details really didn't matter.

"Does this happen for every family?" Tana wondered. "It was really special that he took the time to come and talk to us."

I fully agreed and added, "I wonder if he asked to specifically come and talk to us?" I sometimes put myself in his shoes and wonder if I would be able to go talk to a family that just lost some of their family members, if I was the one to see the aftermath of such a horrific scene.

Tana adamantly stated, "It was something he had to do for himself, and the fact that he was at court and had a victim impact statement speaks volumes."

This part of our conversation was particularly touching for me. As I have for four years now, I thought dearly of Officer Matt as well as all the others on scene that night. Officer Matt has my thoughts and prayers most days, as I simply cannot shake the sight and thought of him holding Miguire's hand as he perhaps was still able to gasp for air or maybe not. Was he full of blood everywhere? I don't really know, and likely don't want to know. These are thoughts that cross my mind often, and every single time I am comforted to know that Officer Matt was there to comfort my favorite little man. That is why I know how important it is for me to send such a great man peace and a healing mind from the things he saw and experienced.

I hesitated before asking the next question. It is still hard to hear the answers every time I ask others about it. I asked, "What do you remember about viewing the bodies?"

Tana said, "I thought, wow, this is really happening. Up until that point we were just told but didn't really have a concrete visual. Ummm…kind of a sense of you know you have to do it but you really don't want to. I always remember the bump on Jordan's head; he just didn't look like himself. I remember it was weird that they still had their winter jackets on." After all, they had died roughly 15 or 16 hours before. We agreed that it is likely the easiest way to prepare a body for viewing when they were pronounced dead at the scene of the accident. Perhaps their jackets never came off.

"Chanda looked exactly how she always did," Tana said emotionally as she recalled what we saw in the viewing room that afternoon. "With her, the only difference was her arm that was up and stiff." It was still in the position it was in after she was extracted from the wreckage. They told us her neck had been snapped on impact, and that her arm was severely broken. Jordan's skull was crushed upon impact, surely causing instant death.

With yet more emotion, Tana reiterated my feelings and thoughts. "The hardest part was watching Mom, her saying goodbye and her words, 'goodbye baby girl'." We both paused for a minute just to let that sit. I am sure we were both right back in that room, seeing and hearing Mom. It is so hard to see people you care about break! To see them crying and feeling so hopeless!

Our conversation stalled for a few minutes as we both needed to collect ourselves again. No matter how many times we think about or talk about the viewing, it is still a very real visual and feeling for us.

Emotions run all over the place and thoughts collide. We were quiet for some time before we could carry on with our conversation.

I then asked Tana, "What do you recall about the house and its contents?"

"They weren't really ours," she answered. "They were Chanda, Jordan, Kamryn and Miguire's. Were there memories of some of the contents? Absolutely! What would have an emotional attachment or memory to it and what wouldn't. I just knew there needed to be a decision made quickly, what was important to keep, and the rest became a formality. As far as the house goes, it was one of the most difficult things to do. I mean, you go from this vibrant home to now it's just four walls. It's only memories; there is no current connection. And for that to happen in five months, from the time we started looking for the will until it was sold," she added emotionally. "And that's a wakeup call to everyone. You work, you spend your life to gain materialistic things, and it's gone in an instant." I agreed that all the things we acquire in our life are just that, THINGS! We are only left with memories in the end.

Tana shared that she was happy when the house was sold and all the contents were given away or sold, along with all the drama that came with it all. The hard feelings between two different families with multiple members involved in a lot of the process. It is never easy, nor is everyone ever happy with the outcome. The best part is when it is all done and gone, and hopefully each person is happy with the couple of items they were able to keep as a memory.

"My biggest lesson in the dealings with the house, its contents, the funeral, and all the things that go along with it all, is to SPEAK one's mind when you want something, disagree with something, or don't feel heard," Tana said. We both shared that it is incredibly hard for the whole process to go smoothly with two families going through such a tragic time.

"What do you remember about the court date?" I asked.

"All I remember was being angry and feeling like Catherine didn't have the guts to look at us or say anything," Tana said. She was referring to the first hearing that happened on the Thursday just two days before the funeral and five days after the tragedy that forever changed us all. Neither of us remember much of this day, as we were all in such shock and fog. Tana spoke of Catherine just being on closed circuit TV rather than being there in person, and that she didn't even look into the camera. I too had been disappointed not to see her in person that day.

My sister shared her curiosity that mirrored some of mine. "I'd be interested to know what she was told to do that day. What does she remember?" She carried on, "My perspective on that day was just angry and disappointed and flabbergasted. It was all Skype and lawyers that knew what was happening, and it was completely misunderstood by us all." Our expectations of what was going to happen and what really happened were so vastly different.

Tana reminded me of the other hearings. I do not remember any of them. My sister went to some of them, but eventually quit going. I do not remember attending any of them, except when Catherine was there in person for sentencing.

"Our meeting with the lawyer, the crown prosecutor was on June 10, 2016," Tana reminded me. "We were getting closer to sentencing. I remember thinking that law has absolutely nothing to do with emotions, and everything is based on previous cases. Our case would be based on another case from Ontario where there were multiple deaths caused." This meeting left Tana feeling as though we had zero say in what would happen in our case. They did ask our opinion, but in the end, we had absolutely zero say in it all.

Then we spoke of the victim impact statements we read in court the day they sentenced Catherine. "I thought our victim impact statements would sway the sentencing in some way, when in fact the sentence was already set between the crown prosecutor and Catherine's lawyer before we arrived." We both agreed that our victim impact statements were the hardest things we have ever done.

Tana shared that her victim impact statement seemed irrelevant at the time we read them. However, about a year later, when she started doing her school presentations about drinking and driving, she pulled most of her presentation from her impact statement. "I am of the opinion that it served no purpose in court, but perhaps it was the first step in my healing process. I poured my heart out when I wrote it and read it out loud in court, and it was incredibly hard on me for quite some time. Looking back on it now, nearly four years later, I choose to see it as perhaps the lowest of days for me in 2016, with nowhere to go but up from there."

Tana recalled how full the courtroom was. "There was only standing room. There were so many people from the news there tweeting as it was happening; it was a high-profile case. Some of Catherine's family were there, and I was happy that they were, because that took guts. That room was full of emotion and victim impact statements about their mom. To hear that…One had to leave if I remember correctly."

She then spoke about the sentencing. "I am sure there are certain points of it I was not mentally there for. It takes a lot of energy and focus. For the most part, you don't want to be there. Leading up to it, you don't know what to expect."

I agreed before venturing into a totally different topic that I had never asked her about, or at least, not that I remembered. "What are your thoughts on the healing lodge?"

"That continues to change," she said. "Initially it was like, what the fuck, how can this be? Only eight months in prison and then moved to the healing lodge. How and why can this be? The whole purpose of the healing lodge is to reintegrate her back into society, leading her life, which will happen. She has the ability to do that mentally, emotionally, physically, and spiritually so that she is whole as a human being, and I get that in my brain, but I am not quite there in my heart." She continued, "It's interesting, the emotions that come up for people when they talk about the healing lodge. Initially, I had a hard time with this and I would avoid it so I wouldn't put my anger about it on others. But I hope she gets the healing she needs because I truly believe that with the work you are doing and the work I am doing, that will collide and be powerful and empowering. If she truly follows what she said in court, she will spend the rest of her life stopping it from happening to others.

Then she could be so powerful herself because who else could be more powerful than someone who was actually behind the wheel?"

She continued, "You think of prison as a place for people who are sick in the brain; psychologically sick. People who have made horrendous, horribly bad decisions consecutively. Vindictive, you know. You think the worst of the worst. We are taught to think that from movies and such. At the end of the day, there are people that are incarcerated because they didn't take care of themselves for 20 to 30 years and didn't make the right decisions for a lot of those years, and that's where she is at. So is the healing lodge the right place for her? She is the only one that can decide that because she is the one in control of her decisions." I agreed with Tana's wise words. I believe this is the case regardless of where someone is incarcerated. We agreed that not having experienced it ourselves, it is very tough to really know what goes on behind bars or behind the walls of any institution that houses criminals, and therefore our opinion is based on very little but assumptions and hearsay.

Next Tana and I talked about the remainder of 2016 once the court proceedings, the house and its contents, and the funeral were behind us. "I kept myself so busy so I didn't have to think," she said. "I went back to my job as a teacher and I threw myself into it. I joined a four-wing band, as I always wanted to do that, and life is short, so why not do what I am passionate about?" She recounted, "I took myself out of that whole seven months and put it away in a compartment in the back of my brain. I went back to a job that was completely and totally supportive, and I think that is very important for people to know. I didn't go to a job where people had high expectations of me. They knew things were not normal. They all helped me; the kids helped me. I wouldn't have been able to do it without them. They were my family and still are!" Tana continued to share with emotion in her voice. "They helped me get my focus back. January, February, and March were a complete write-off for me. I didn't start to come back until about May or June. I just really compartmentalized what happened and did not integrate it yet. I would take that box out when I was ready."

I didn't say much as I listened to my eldest sister share her memories of the hardest year of our lives. She said, "Christmas and Thanksgiving were the hardest part of the latter half of 2016. Then, leading into 2017 was the first anniversary of the accident, which was a whole other ball of yuckiness." Tana conveyed that she had a very restless night the day of the anniversary, which amounted to no sleep at all. Her sheer anger was boiling over for a few different reasons, one of them being the media coverage that was front and center on the one-year anniversary. I chose not to say anything more about the topic.

Tana shared that 2016 brought "many days where I just sat on the couch in a daze with the TV on and James sitting next to me. But for the most part, I slept pretty well," she added. "Unless I knew I had something big to do like clean stuff out of Chanda's house or maybe going through her Mary Kay inventory, the nights before those events caused some sleeplessness." She shared with me that it always helped when she had people there to help with those difficult tasks. It certainly made it easier to cope and she would forever remember that. "The majority of the year was a daze, and it was like I was a child again to put some perspective on it," she continued.

When I asked Tana how things changed and evolved after 2016, when the grief fog was somewhat lifted, she reiterated, "I think the biggest difference is I have taken that box out and re-integrated it, and I knew I could put them together more than I could before." She was referring to the fact that she had to compartmentalize things during 2016 that she was unable to deal with at that time. As a school teacher, she decided to do a presentation in her social classes. "In my head I knew I could connect to the curriculum. I wasn't even thinking past Goodsoil (the school she taught in). Getting permission to do that in my grade 7 and 8 class and how it looked, and then presenting it to the staff to get that permission; and once that happened, the doors opened. And so I had a focus that allowed me to speak my story and feel like I could have an impact," she said proudly. "That's what changed everything!"

We chatted about having a positive focus after the tragedy and how important it had been for us both in our healing journey. Finding a way to openly talk about and share our experience had been extremely rewarding for us both. "Internal is that focus piece; something to do with that tragedy, and external is all the support you get." She proceeded to list off family members who had fully supported her in her efforts. "The amazing response from the teachers and adults that hear it is what keeps you going, and the conversations that you have with students…suicide and…my dad's an alcoholic and we are scared every night he leaves that he is not coming back and what damage he is doing," she shared, referring to some very real conversations she had with other people.

I listened with pride as she told me, "To go from proving to your principal that this is a good thing to being at the national conference in two months…that's wow! And still raw; my presentation was not professional at all at that point, but they were willing to listen to the content. Tana shared that she knew she would be doing this for the rest of her life. "It's interesting how it evolves depending on the decisions you make," she said. "How we react to things that happen in our life is a choice." Despite another presenter picking apart Tana's presentation, saying it was poorly done and that it needed a handful of major changes, she pushed on and kept doing more. It isn't about putting on a big show. People want real and raw, and that is what they get from both Tana and myself when we talk about drinking and driving and the effects it has on everyone.

The tragedy is not Tana's main focus. "I needed to find balance, and everyone balances differently," she said. "I haven't made the tragedy my full focus. It's not my full life. I don't think I could make it my main focus because then you are in that headspace all the time, whereas if you have other things of importance in your life it's more balanced. I still compartmentalize. It's just easier to bring it out every time; that intensity is not the same." We agreed that the balance needs to be a constant, daily practice.

We also agreed that with balance comes a responsibility to look after ourselves. It isn't up to someone else to do it for us. I said "There are still days when I am in it and go there, I absolutely do. The important part is that it is minutes or hours and not days, weeks, or months." Tana agreed, and we spoke of the fact that we are proud of each other for the constant work we have put into ourselves. It is and will be exciting to see how this all plays out. I know for a fact that Chanda is always looking down with a guiding smile, leading us in the right direction.

Finally, we spoke of our family unit. Tana said, "When we lost Chanda, we lost our cohesiveness!" There really is no other word to best describe Chanda. She was the glue that held us all together, and that togetherness is forever changed. "Now we are left purposely and intentionally making decisions together. It's not as simple anymore." It is very tough to put into words how something like this changes a family forever.

Victim's Name: Tana Deibert

Police Service: Warman RCMP

Offence Date: Sunday, January 3, 2016

Offence Location: Intersection of HWY 11 and Wanuskewin Road

Incident/File Number:

I have been pushed beyond "being comfortable, being uncomfortable" on many personal levels. The Emotional Impact of this family tragedy cannot be justifiably explained with single words. Words are not enough. Therefore, I would like you to visualize the following memories, descriptions, comparisons and contrasts. I apologize for any painful memories that may return to all family members and friends. However, I feel it is absolutely necessary to be a poignant voice for Chanda, Jordan, Kamryn, and Miguire. All four of these human beings were individuals with true personalities.

Miguire was a sweet little boy who loved to analyze the workings of toys. The last living memory I have of Miguire is playing with the Go! Go! Smart Wheels Racing Set James and I gave him for Christmas. With excitement, his Dad, Jordan, set up the race track up downstairs in Grandma Marie's basement. I'm not sure who was more excited, Jordan or Miguire! Miguire crouched down following the car around the entire track while pushing the button to will the car to go faster. He tried to figure out the relationship with the button on the remote and the speed of the car by slowing down, stopping, speeding up. On Friday, January 1, 2016, Chanda text me, "By the way, the batteries are done on our remote controller which means it is well used". They played hard; the gift was well played with for exactly one week! Excitement, happiness, and Christmas spirit was all around. 2.5 yrs earlier, on Saturday, September 7, 2013, a beautiful baby boy was welcomed into this world. I had the personal honour of being Miguire's first visitor other than his Mom and Dad. It was a joy to hold him, cuddle him, kiss him while swaddled tightly in a hospital baby blanket. In stark contrast, on Sunday, January 3, 2016, Miguire, $2\frac{1}{3}$ yrs old, was once again swaddled tightly in a hospital blanket. The RCMP had told us Miguire hadn't a chance to recover from his

Victim's Name: Tana Deibert

Police Service: Warman RCMP

Offence Date: Sunday, January 3, 2016

Offence Location: Intersection of HWY 11 and Wanuskewin Road

Incident/File Number:

injuries. Why was he being held by a family member in Kamryn's room? I wasn't prepared; I was numb; my breath completely taken away. It was time to hold the lifeless, breathless baby Miguire and kiss him for one last time. No eye contact with the beautiful blue eyes, no mischievous look, no smiles, no giggles, no hockey. He is gone! Just sheer shock, agony, and devastation. What is the reason I am saying goodbye so very soon? What would have this intelligent little boy, Miguire David Louis Van de Vorst, done in life? How would he have impacted lives in the future? What descriptive words, feelings, and emotions come to your mind?

My last living memory of Kamryn is a two person dance party at Uncle Chad's house. The room was filled with music, laughter, giggles, and, of course, awesome dance moves. Oh, the giggles and oh, the endless energy of a five year old. We were having an absolute blast!!! In stark contrast, on Sunday, January 3, 2016, exactly one week later, my eyes saw a very different picture. Kamryn, my once vibrant niece, was laying still on a hospital bed. Completely unresponsive! She was being kept alive with life support. She was being kept warm with warming blankets. Her hair full with dry blood. The nurses having to continuously suction and clean secretions. By late morning, the diagnosis was official. Kamryn is brain dead! Not brain damage, but brain death! Kamryn will also succumb to the impact of the collision. Then the decision of organ and tissue decision commenced. Once again, I wasn't prepared; I was numb; my breath completely taken away. Our beautiful flower girl gone from our lives. May her heart live long. What would this intelligent little girl, Kamryn Niley Marie Van de Vorst, done in life? How would she have impacted lives? Once again I ask what descriptive words, feelings, and emotions come to your mind?

Victim's Name: Tana Deibert

Police Service: Warman RCMP

Offence Date: Sunday, January 3, 2016

Offence Location: Intersection of HWY 11 and Wanuskewin Road

Incident/File Number:

Chanda, my younger sister by seven years, was the glue or cohesiveness to our family. She was forever planning simple events to gather immediate and extended family. James and I fondly knick-named her the coordinator. From a young age Chanda captivated my heart. My heart overflowed with love for the little white-haired girl with smiles from ear to ear. We shared a bedroom for as long as we remained under Mom and Dad's roof. We knew each other so well, we frequently answered community member's questions about each other. We forever got mixed up. So, I answered questions about hockey and she answered questions about music and teaching. Mom, do you remember Chanda and I waking you and Dad up at 6:00a.m. daily with our skipping ropes hitting the concrete outside your bedroom window and the giggles? This routine was our warm-up for weight training. Chanda would later struggle with deciding to become either an Exercise Therapist or a Physical Education teacher within the school system. As I am a teacher, we had many discussions over the advantages and disadvantages of teaching. Her official occupation became an exercise therapist BUT I have learnt since the tragedy that she truly was a teacher as well. Chanda was a constant support for many clients, friends, and family. Her compassion for people was never-ending. We created and presented "To the Bride" speeches at each other's weddings. Many of you here today were present at Chanda and Jordan's wedding. Visualize her wearing her wedding gown, the orange lilies, the smiles, the family pictures. Remember the excitement around their trip to Iceland; remember the joy shared with Jordan's photography; remember the videos and pictures of the Aurora, tobogganing and first skating experiences. Now visualize Chanda lying on a gurney in the family room of the hospital basement. She still has her winter coat on and she looks exactly like the Chanda I know and love. She looks the same with one exception. Her right arm is

Victim's Name: Tana Deibert

Police Service: Warman RCMP

Offence Date: Sunday, January 3, 2016

Offence Location: Intersection of HWY 11 and Wanuskewin Road

Incident/File Number:

stiffly placed upright above her head. An automatic reaction that cannot be changed. Now visualize watching and listening to your Mom strongly saying, "Goodbye my Baby Girl!" Another vividly distinct moment I wasn't prepared for; I was numb; my breath completely taken away. Once again, I ask what descriptive words, feelings, and emotions come to your mind? When I choose to let myself, I inconsolably weep.

These gut wrenching, vivid memories are only of the first immediate day of the tragedy. Then followed the challenging formal tasks of organizing the funeral, changing the Van de Vorst home to an empty house and dispersing contents, creating the gravestone, court appearances, lawyers appointments, and writing a Victim Impact Statement. All of these important tasks completed by two distinct families - different personalities, different systems, different ways of grieving....with the same goal in mind. These examples are far from an exhaustive list. I thank all family whom have supported each other through this process.

How has the senseless impaired driving incident on Sunday, January 3, 2016 affected my life? Two months later when our grandson, Jaxon Michael Deibert, was born 16.5 wks premature, instead of turning right into the Pediatric Intensive Care Unit, we turned left into the Neonatal Intensive Care Unit. The same floor, the same hallway of RUH. This familiarity created excruciating agitation. All of the first 40 hour memories would instantaneously rush back. I stuffed down my triggers of sadness and visited for the three weeks of his life anyway. Yes, more devastation and death! I did not drive for three months (a decision not consciously made). When I started to drive, I instinctively looked at every intersection I drove by which made a four hour drive to Goodsoil from Saskatoon extremely exhausting. I have not played piano (my passion and major in

Victim's Name: Tana Deibert

Police Service: Warman RCMP

Offence Date: Sunday, January 3, 2016

Offence Location: Intersection of HWY 11 and Wanuskewin Road

Incident/File Number:

university) since the funeral and my Kindergarten classes no longer sing Twinkle, Twinkle Little Star and ABC. For three months, I felt sheer mental, physical, emotional, and spiritual exhaustion, and the lack of ability to focus for more than two hours. I missed fifty four days of teaching directly related to this tragedy. Every student and staff member at Goodsoil Central School were impacted by the severity of losing an entire family of four! Some emotions that immediately come to mind include unimaginable, incomprehensible, heart-wrenching, profound loss, disbelief, deep sadness, grief stricken, an inescapable whole in our family, trauma, devastation, exhaustion, humbling, unfathomable, surreal, intense, searching and seeking for answers, needless and avoidable. The loss of Chanda, Jordan, Kamryn, and Miguire has deeply affected my daily life. I struggle with the word and concept of peace. I struggle with peace and forgiveness versus hatred. I struggle with any miniscule morsel of empathy and sympathy. I have been pushed beyond "being comfortable, being uncomfortable" on many personal levels. On a daily basis, I am purposefully and intentionally working towards creating my new normal, my new happiness. My husband simply requests, "I want my wife back".

SCHOOL TALKS WITH SADD AND MADD WITH TANA

TANA STARTED SHARING our family's story in schools and at conferences. Again, the Mierau feminine strength was shining through her in big ways. As of today, she has delivered 31 amazing experiences for students across Saskatchewan as well as Alberta, sharing our family tragedy in order to influence young people to consider their actions when it comes to drinking and driving.

I had the privilege of hearing her speak on three such occasions. She named her presentation 'Tribute of Love', and it has had wonderful reviews. Teachers and students alike praise her for one of the best presentations of its kind, including those that have heard other presentations for 30 plus years.

On one particular occasion, Tana was presenting at the SADD (Students Against Drunk Driving) conference in Saskatoon in the fall of 2017, and I had the privilege of attending along with Tana's husband James, my mom, and my youngest son Hudson. It was the first time I was able to take it in, and wow, was I ever impressed. It was a little bit eerie at first as the three of us sat at the back of the room while Tana opened up her presentation with slides and stories. She introduced us and all the high school students along with their respective teachers looked to the back of the room. I could feel the empathy and compassion in the room. It was very surreal! I shed tears, as did my mom and at one point even Hudson too.

I was filled with emotion. I was so proud of Tana for having the strength and courage to stand in front of a few hundred students and adults to share our family's tragedy in the hope of making an impact on others to make better choices for themselves and their friends and families. At times, the entire room was completely silent. At others, we heard sniffles and tears, and even outbursts of crying.

It simply was amazing how many students and teachers came up to us and thanked us for coming to support Tana and allowing them to hear our story. Some of the teachers also thanked us, and multiple people said it was the best or one of the best presentations they had ever heard. I made contact with a few of the teachers there and still remain connected to them three years later.

We left the SADD conference with great pride for the wonderful job Tana had done. I was so happy that I was able to attend my first SADD presentation. The adrenaline that had been running through Tana's veins for hours, if not days, had her bouncing around like a little girl on Christmas morning. After the presentation she shared that she usually did not sleep much after her presentations as it gets her amped up and full of emotion. I definitely could understand how that can happen.

In my heart I know for a fact that this has and is a large part of Tana's healing journey. She shares deeply and emotionally in front of her audience in a very profound way. I too shed tears along with others when I attended, and oh, how powerful her words are!

It's harsh to see the pictures of my family onscreen when Tana is doing her presentations, yet I am filled with pride knowing Chanda, Jordan, Kamryn, and Miguire are making a difference. In a way, it feels like not all is lost. They still live on through a powerful message. A message of strength and courage like never before. I cannot begin to share the right words to show just how much pride and admiration I have for Tana for having the strength and courage to share her words in front of so many attentive crowds of eager-to-learn youngsters.

Much like my mom, Tana too has this abundant strength and determination to serve others in the most heartfelt ways possible. As a school teacher, she has done so on a daily basis, teaching the curriculum to her students. Sharing her heart's biggest hole and scars with others in a very intimate and vulnerable way is beyond courageous and admirable. There are no words. I am filled with pride and smiles when I think of her relentless giving.

Together Forever

Van de Vorst

Jordan, Chanda, Kamryn, Miguire

Jordan Lee Van de Vorst, 34, his wife, Chanda Marie (nee Mierau), 33, and their two young children, Kamryn Niley Marie, 5 and Miguire David Louis, 2, passed away tragically on Sunday, January 3rd. Jordan is survived by his parents, Lou and Linda Van de Vorst; siblings Angie White (Shenton) and their children Sebela and Avaya, Joel Van de Vorst (Chandra) and Alyssa Van de Vorst. Chanda is predeceased by her father, Elmer Mierau; and survived by her mother, Marie Mierau; and sister Tana Deibert (James) and their children, Kyla, Logan, Kelan, and Ashley; her brother Tyler Mierau (Chandra) and their children Zairyn, Samuel, and Logan; and her brother Chad Mierau (Melanie) and their children, Sage, Hudson, Derek, Carter and Karlie. The family is also survived by numerous grandparents, uncles, aunts, and cousins.

Jordan and Chanda began their journey together in Saskatoon, playing hockey at the University of Saskatchewan while studying in their respective fields of Science. In 2005, Chanda graduated with a Bachelor of Science in Kinesiology while Jordan graduated the same year with a Bachelor of Science, specializing in Microbiology and Immunology. After briefly residing in Whitewood, Weyburn and Moose Jaw they had relocated to Saskatoon to plant their roots. They were married on June 6, 2009 and on June 28, 2010 welcomed their daughter, Kamryn, into the world. Kamryn was brilliant; she had an extraordinary personality and contagious smile that enhanced the lives of those who were lucky enough to have met her. Three years later, on September 7th, their family grew larger, once more, with the birth of their son, Miguire. Their little man rounded out their family unit, balancing the scales, and offsetting the number of the barbies and high-heels with trucks and action figures. Together, the foursome shared a passion for life that was admired by all who knew them. Their days were spent together, making the most out of each moment, no matter how small. Jordan and Chanda devoted their lives to their children and in return, their lives were made whole by Kamryn and Miguire, a love that was evident to all who crossed paths with them. The family continues their journey together in the heavens as well as in the legacy they have left behind.

The family would like to thank the first responders, the staff at RUH, and the transplant teams for their incredible compassion and care during this difficult time.

Memorial Donations
Pediatric Intensive Care Unit at RUH or Teddy Bears Anonymous

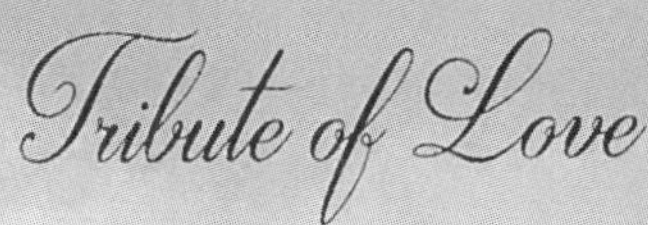

Saturday, January 9, 2016 ~ 11:00 a.m.
Elim Church ~ Saskatoon, SK

Presider ~ Pastor Marvin Wojda

Pianist ~ JoAnne Fredlund

Piano Prelude

Welcome ~ Pastor Marvin

The Scriptures ~ Doug Schultz

"Amazing Grace" ~ Congregation

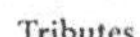

Tributes
Jodi Martens ~ Tribute to Chanda
Joel, Angie and Alyssa ~ Tribute to Jordan
Lori Barsi ~ Tribute to Kamryn and Miguire

Choir ~ Joy of Vox
"Angel On The Roof" and "Borders and Time"

Slide Presentation ~ Jacqui and Mike from
Saskatchewan Aurora Hunters & Saskatchewan Freedom Photography

Piano solo ~ Tana Deibert
"Fly" by Celine Dion

Meditation ~ Pastor Marvin

"In the Garden" ~ Congregation

Benediction ~ Pastor Marvin

Congregation Led By Auntie Tana
"Twinkle, Twinkle" and "A,B,C,D..."

"Time for Kisses and Hugs"

Piano Processional

To everything there is a season, and a time
to every purpose under the heaven;
a time to be born, and a time to die; a time to plant,
and a time to pluck up that
which is planted;
a time to kill, and a time to heal, a time
to break down, and a time to build up;
a time to weep, and a time to laugh, a time to mourn,
and a time to dance;
a time to cast away stones, and a time
to gather stones together; a time to embrace, and a time to
refrain from embracing;
a time to get, and a time to lose; a time
to keep, and a time to cast away;
a time to rend, and a time to sew; a time to keep silence,
and a time to speak;
a time to love, and a time to hate; a
time of war and a time of peace.

Ecclesiastes 3:1-8

MOURNING GLORY
FUNERAL AND CREMATION SERVICES
(306) 978-5200

Photo taken by Jordan Van de Vorst

WALK WITH ME

ON A WARM, sunny day in August 2016, I was at the graveyard in Saskatoon. I went to see Chanda and Jordan and the kids, and I specifically remember a nice new shiny train passing by. I smiled and thought to myself that Miguire would sure have loved to see that. The breeze was warm and the sun was shining bright. The bunny rabbit that visited occasionally was there that day, aimlessly wandering around the part of the cemetery that I was in.

I sat down on the ground and stared at their headstone, confused and lost. I had been there quite a few times before, almost always alone. And each time it seemed as though I was piecing together thoughts and still trying to make sense of it all. On this particular day, I was uneasy as I sat there. Something felt different. I didn't know what or why, I just knew that something was different.

I was unable to focus on the gravestone. Suddenly I had a gut feeling or an instinct, or maybe intuition. I'm not really sure what it was. I found myself standing up and starting to walk, but not really with any direction. I followed the bunny across the grass for a while. It veered off into a bush and I kept walking across the cemetery.

I had never ventured anywhere else in that cemetery other than where their gravestone was. This was new territory for me. Something was leading me to explore. I think this was the first time I was at the cemetery that I was actually able to see the things that I had missed before. Areas that I didn't know even existed, weirdly shaped trees that I never noticed before, and a pond with a water geyser. There was a beautiful wooden bridge arched over the pond.

As I approached the pond, I was pleasantly surprised to see swans swimming in it. There were about a dozen just effortlessly floating about in the water. There were ripples in the water from the swans swimming as well as from the water spraying up into the air.

I thoroughly enjoyed my time at the pond, but still I was curious. What was leading me there? What was it that I was supposed to see or do? I decided that I had been led there just to see the pond and recognize that there are beautiful things on the side of the cemetery that I hadn't seen before. I hung out in this area for perhaps 10 or 15 minutes, enjoying the sights and hearing the sounds. I believe it was the first time that I felt such peace and calmness since the accident.

I then started to head back towards the Van De Vorst gravestone. I walked slowly, enjoying the warm sun, feeling the warm breeze and just being. It was wonderful to finally feel that again. It had eluded me for so long. I was enjoying it so much that I found myself walking incredibly slowly, stopping at trees just to look and gaze, noticing the butterflies floating about.

About a third of the way back, next to a tree right against the road, I found myself frozen in my tracks. An overwhelming sense of coolness flooded my body from head to toe. As the chill consumed me, I found my eyes closing. I'm not so sure I had ever felt that calm before in my life. I really had no idea what was happening; this was a very new experience for me.

The sensations in my body led right to the bottom of my fingertips. I stretched out my arms, hands wide open, fingers reaching to the ground. Then I felt the most amazing feeling I had ever felt. There was a warm feeling on the very tip of the index finger on my right hand. I stayed frozen; incredibly calm, my mind at ease. The warm feeling on my index finger put a smile on my face, a very, very big smile.

A small set of fingers were clenching my index finger. Warm fingers; ever so tiny. There was no mistaking that Miguire was holding my finger. Once I realized what was happening, the intensity of the chill in my body subsided. I slowly opened my eyes, still feeling those tiny little fingers wrapped around my finger. There was a gentle tug.

With complete elation, I took a small step forward as if to follow the direction I was being tugged in. Once I took that first step, the pull on my finger became less urgent. My entire body was filled with an incredible warmth. My favorite little man and I walked ever so slowly across the cemetery. I shuffled along slowly and aimlessly; it felt completely perfect. Miguire's tiny little hand holding my finger warmed me from top to bottom, inside and out. As we walked, I suddenly understood why I was being led across the cemetery. I knew then that Miguire had been waiting for me. He was there to comfort me and to walk with me just one more time. For the first time in my life, I experienced something that I had only read about or seen in movies. Miguire's spirit was right next to me somehow!

There is no other explanation for what happened. There is no way to make sense of it, and I don't much care to. I am just super grateful to have had the experience of whatever that was with Miguire at the cemetery that day. I haven't a clue how long we walked for, nor do I know how far we went. I just know that he and I walked back to his eternal resting place.

My little man lifted my spirits and calmed my soul that day. He warmed my heart, and it was exactly what I needed amongst all the chaos that had been going on.

Upon arriving at the grave again, I sat down and I wept. For the first time that year, I cried with a smile on my face. There were no words between us, and I didn't look down. It was a surreal moment in time that I chose not to change in any way. For just a second, I consciously thought "I can't look down. I don't know what I'll see." I knew for sure that it was Miguire. I knew the touch of his hand. It was the feeling of the hand that I had felt many, many times before.

Thoughts of complete joy and endless happiness flooded through my mind as I cried like a baby. I smiled from ear to ear as I continued taking it in; indescribable feelings I had never felt before. A new experience I never thought possible.

I left the cemetery that day with a smile on my face and a spring in my step that I had been missing for quite some time. That day was and always will be one of my favorite days ever. Without that day, I'm not sure how I would have made it through 2016.

Not long after that day in the cemetery, a good friend of mine, Anthony, reached out to me and he shared with me that Miguire's spirit was at the local bowling alley. On December 27, 2015, the Mierau family had a Christmas get-together at the bowling alley in our local town. It was one of the last days that we got to see Chanda, Jordan, Kamryn, and Miguire.

I went to see Anthony, and he and I had sat in front of lane three in the bowling alley to reminisce and remember the day we had there with the kids. That was where I had shown Miguire to sit on his bum with his legs apart and to push that big giant bowling ball towards the pins as hard as he could. Anthony told me about Miguire being around when he was there and shared some of the things that were happening there when the bowling alley was closed.

For the next six months or so, I would go to lane three to sit with Miguire. Most times I sat in that lane in 2016, there were other people in the room. Sometimes Anthony, sometimes other people. It didn't matter to me, as I was there to see Miguire or at least feel his presence. Anthony and I both knew when he was no longer there in spirit.

Even to this day when I go to the bowling alley, I still go to lane three and spend just a few moments or maybe longer just to remember. It makes me wonder whether Miguire is present. Whether other people have felt his presence. I don't really know for sure, all I know is that I'm super grateful to have had those experiences with Miguire.

THE DEEPEST PAIN CAN OFFER THE BIGGEST GROWTH

THROUGH THE MOST painful experience of my life has come the most amazing growth journey that I never dreamed would happen. As I ponder how to best describe my innermost thoughts and heart-centered feelings, I am pulled to the times I have been able to sit face-to-face with Spenny, Parker, and Kayla. It brings me to tears knowing that I was able to do that in a profound way. Now, in 2020, I find myself editing and completing a book that I feel will surely help thousands of people, if not millions. To reflect on the past four years is very odd in many ways. Instantly I think, how is this all a reality? Did this all actually happen?

I must sit here and dig deep with gratitude. I feel a purpose like never before. I was led to do this for a reason, and not just to help others. The conversations I had with the McKay family were nothing short of amazing—sharing tears, hugs, and over a short period of time, love! It is all incredibly amazing to me.

I recall the times I went to see Kayla at the bakery and how wonderful that felt for me, and I am curious if she felt the same way. Two strangers coming together from the opposite sides of such a horrific story. Spenny and I, meeting in his garage the first time. He was hesitant, quiet, and reserved, as was I. We were both treading lightly to see what the other person would say or do. I cannot help but smile considering how it all turned out and how it's still going.

The way I see it is that this is only the beginning. I hold a strong belief that Catherine and I will be talking face-to-face soon in the most extraordinary way; sharing our experiences with each other and striving towards a common goal of educating the general public about drinking and driving and the effects it has on families.

To outsiders looking in, it might seem strange that I formed lifelong friendships with the McKays, growing and healing together. There are periods of time when Spenny and I communicate daily. Other times we don't speak at all for a few weeks at a time, yet the love and understanding between us is always there, whether we're talking about work, our kids, our spouses, or anything in-between. Of course we also talk about how his mom is doing now that she is out on day parole, because I am always curious how she is doing.

There really is nothing profound about all this other than the fact that I choose to deal with it head-on. I took what was a devastating event in my life and chose to better understand how everyone else was and is feeling or doing. It is my belief that there is a disconnect in today's society. People are not staying deeply connected with those around them. Communication is lacking, love is lost, and there is no understanding. It all starts with being open and vulnerable.

In September of 2019, I went to a ranch in California for a personal development course. That was the first time I spoke of this burning desire to share my story in the form of a book. Much to my surprise, a woman who I had met just 18 months earlier was in tears standing next to me when I was sharing this desire with the group. She then shared that, as a toddler, she lost her dad in a drunk-driving accident. She was very emotional just listening to me share. I knew then that this had to be done.

We have a responsibility in this ever-changing world to help people connect in some way, whether it be with something from their past or something that is happening in their life now. It could be an event, or a person, or a thing. I just know there needs to be more connection.

As I write this and the world is working its way through unprecedented times with Covid-19 and the effects it has had on human connection, it is even more apparent to me that we all need to forgive, understand, and communicate out of love more than ever.

I put myself in Catherine's shoes and imagine her upbringing; how her life played out to the point that she ended up in prison for killing four other people, and it sure makes me think differently than I ever have. Similarly I wonder, how do others become drug addicts or murderers? How do people get to the point they want to commit suicide? How can I understand other people currently in my life that may just need someone to care enough so they don't have another drink, or they don't feel the need to commit suicide, or they don't feel all alone in this sometimes cruel world? I understand someone's past cannot be an excuse for their actions, but I do think with some humility and grace we can help rebuild and help those that are seemingly headed down the wrong life path.

It is my responsibility to take the time to help those around me. Family, friends, coworkers, employees, tenants, strangers, and anyone else I come across on a daily basis. Without a doubt, if we all did this society would be much healthier. That is why I choose this every day. I don't profess to have all the answers, I just feel that if we understand those that hurt us most just for a second, we would realize that we are all very alike. Regardless of our background, race, or religion, we are all in this together.

Hurting hearts turned to healing hearts can make a huge difference in other people's lives. We have all been hurt in many different ways, and I would suggest that we all have the ability to help others get through the things we have been through. Empathy and compassion go a very long way when we reach out to others. Heart-centered caring for others has a healing quality that is undeniable. The question is, who is willing to share so openly with those around them? I have, and I will forever continue to do so, as it has been most rewarding in every way. With a full heart I can honestly say that this tragedy has shaped me into a better human being in every single way. Initially it was a choice, and now it is the norm!

ALL IS WELL

AS I SIT at my desk on December 31, 2020, listening to the sound of rain falling while I edit and contemplate my book, I can't help but smile. I am full of pride, happiness, and joy.

Due to Covid-19, only a small portion of our family celebrated Christmas this year, with all the usual food and late nights like we always do. For me though, this year has been very different, and in a good way.

My heart is full of love. I can honestly say that I love the holiday season again, and I am able to celebrate all that Christmas means to me and my family. Oh, it is such an amazing feeling. Mom seems to be doing well, as are Tana and James, Angie, and all our kids. My once-shattered heart seems to be doing very well, in fact, this was the first Christmas in 15 years that I loved it all again. For so many years, I felt like I closed my eyes and tried to make it through the holiday season with the least amount of pain possible. For so many years, I felt only the broken heart, the loss, and the indescribable pain.

No more. Those days are finally in the past. I have been spending more and more time coaching or talking to others about their past traumas and pains. It is extremely exciting to feel so good and very much ready to push forward helping others. I have become proficient at being open and vulnerable in conversations with people, and that has opened up a tremendous amount of doors for me to explore in the future.

There is no telling what lies ahead, but I do know that it is exciting and exhilarating to feel so ready for it, no matter what direction it takes me in. I am pleased with the things I have created; things that are still in their infancy stages. I am all geared towards helping other people to find their inner peace. I know that what I have learned about myself and how I have been able to navigate through such a challenging time in my life will serve me well as I work towards helping others achieve the same in their lives.

My friend Anthony passed away while I was writing this book. Before he passed, he agreed that I could share the stories of the bowling alley in my book. Anthony was a man who continuously gave of himself in the hope of helping those around him as best he could. I will continue to do the good things he was always doing. Shortly after Anthony passed away, I created a Facebook group called Lane 3 in his honor, and I foresee a coaching and support system following in the next little while, all with the same intent to help others figure out a way to deal with the hard things in life.

I can't help but smile as I think about the fact that losing some of my favorite people in my life has actually made me so incredibly strong. My father Elmer, good friend Dan Schultz, Chanda, Jordan, Kamryn, Miguire, and most recently Anthony. All these amazing people, gone too soon. What once caused me unfathomable pain has actually ended up making me stronger and has driven me to reach as many people as I can in a positive way.

To think, right now during the holiday season between Christmas and New Year's, I am finishing up my book and feeling amazing about it all. Yet even a year ago, I had to put it all down as I simply could not deal with the hurt and pain I was still holding on to. Life is wonderful again. In fact, it always has been, I just did not see it at the time.

Reflecting back on this journey, I consider what worked for me. It started with forgiveness for myself, followed by forgiveness for others. This opened up my entire being again. I really feel like I am now able to leave the past pain behind while still remembering all the cherished memories from the past. Truly, this has and will continue to create inner peace and well-being. I sincerely hope that by being so open and sharing my story and Catherine's family's story, others will also find some healing. Even perhaps forgiveness. Just one person, or maybe a few thousand or more.

Please share our story with anyone you know who might gain some insight from it and apply it to their own lives. Be kind to one another, and always lead with love, compassion, and empathy. I know how powerful these tools have been for me, and I trust they can be just as useful and powerful for others as well.

Always remember, how we react to situations in our life is a choice. Furthermore, how we treat other people is always a choice. Most importantly, be kind to yourself. Take a second to have a look in the mirror and give yourself a big pat on the back. Offer yourself some grace; a little bit of acceptance. You will be amazed at how well you do with a little self-assurance.

Finally, to those of you who previously could not allow yourself to think positively about the things that happened in your life, try again. I can attest to the fact that once I dealt with my inner demons and self-destructive thoughts and issues, I began to see everything else in a different light. Yes, even things I had thought so negatively about for many years. How I see myself is how I see others! Period.

Now, it is as though there is nothing out there that can negatively impact me long-term. Yes, perhaps it would impact me for minutes, hours, or a few days, but not for months, years, and decades like it once did. In a way, it seems I have the ability to fast-track the negative feelings and figure a way through them while holding on to the positives for much, much longer. Oh, how good it feels.

There are a few things I would like to touch on just briefly. Generally speaking, there are some instances where my version of events differ slightly from Tana's version of the same events. The same goes for any events relayed to me by Kayla or any of her family members and mine. I did not change these in my book, as I wrote them purely according to each person's perceptions or recollections.

One very important (or not) discrepancy is the Toyota emblem I picked up from the crash site in early 2016. I learned near the end of 2020 that Catherine's vehicle was not a Toyota at all, but rather a Jeep Wrangler Rubicon. I was incredibly upset with myself when I learned this, yet I decided to not edit that out of the book or change it. My mind obviously missed that fact or something. I do not have an explanation, but I will say this. That emblem, even though it is not from either vehicle, still holds the same value for me as it always has. Yes, I got some facts wrong; it's only natural given the circumstances we were going through. In the end, I decided I needed to follow my own advice and give myself some grace and forgiveness. It does not change anything. I was still there multiple times, cleaning up the ditch. It does not matter that some of the items may have been from previous accidents at the same corner.

Be gentle in your judgments, especially to yourself. Be kind in your daily life, graceful towards others, and love those you love even harder. Live each day to its fullest as though it is your last, while caring for others like it is the hardest day of their entire life. Take chances, experience things you normally would not, give when you normally would take, allow yourself to receive when others are wanting to give. Open your heart to strangers, stay with friends a little longer, sleep more once in a while, find your passion and WHY, do what seems impossible. And, as they say, be all that you can be without hesitation.

I am here for you. Reach out if you want or need to. And do the same for others!

LANE 3 CONSULTING

The name Lane 3 has so lovingly stuck with me and has led me to launching a few new programs for us to stay connected.

I am beyond excited to help as many people as I can and would love to provide the opportunity for anyone to reach me. Lane 3 Consulting is my newest passion that will allow me to truly give and serve others. More importantly Lane 3 Foundation will be my way of giving back. As these are both very much in their infancy stages I trust you will all be excited and optimistic with the opportunities to work together going forward.

All throughout the process of writing this book I have had a website up for people to read about what my book is about and to purchase a pre-sale copy. Now that my book has launched, I will keep my website up and running for a place to have people reach out to me as well as release details about the new programs.

www.survivingthecrash.co
saskychad@gmail.com
lanethreeconsulting@gmail.com

Jordan, Chanda, Kamryn, Miguire Van de Vorst

Jordan Lee Van de Vorst, 34, his wife, Chanda Marie (nee Mierau), 33, and their two young children, Kamryn Niley Marie, 5 and Miguire David Louis, 2, passed away tragically on Sunday, January 3rd. Jordan is survived by his parents, Lou and Linda Van de Vorst; siblings Angie White (Shenton) and their children Sebela and Avaya, Joel Van de Vorst (Chandra) and Alyssa Van de Vorst. Chanda is predeceased by her father, Elmer Mierau; and survived by her mother, Marie Mierau; and sister Tana Deibert (James) and their children, Kyla, Logan, Kelan, and Ashley; her brother Tyler Mierau (Chandra) and their children Zairyn, Samuel, and Logan; and her brother Chad Mierau (Melanie) and their children, Sage, Hudson, Derek, Carter and Karlie. The family is also survived by numerous grandparents, uncles, aunts, and cousins. Jordan and Chanda began their journey together in Saskatoon, playing hockey at the University of Saskatchewan while studying in their respective fields of Science. In 2005, Chanda graduated with a Bachelor of Science in Kinesiology while Jordan graduated the same year with a Bachelor of Science, specializing in Microbiology & Immunology. After briefly residing in Whitewood, Weyburn and Moose Jaw they had relocated to Saskatoon to plant their roots. They were married on June 6, 2009 and on June 28, 2010 welcomed their daughter, Kamryn, into the world. Kamryn was brilliant; she had an extraordinary personality and contagious smile that enhanced the lives of those who were lucky enough to have met her. Three years later, on September 7th, their family grew larger, once more, with the birth of their son, Miguire. Their little man rounded out their family unit, balancing the scales, and offsetting the number of the barbies and high-heels with trucks and action figures. Together, the foursome shared a passion for life that was admired by all who knew them. Their days were spent together, making the most out of each moment, no matter how small. Jordan and Chanda devoted their lives to their children and in return, their lives were made whole by Kamryn and Miguire, a love that was evident to all who crossed paths with them. The family continues their journey together in the heavens as well as in the legacy they have left behind.

A Tribute of Love was held at 11:00 a.m. on Saturday, January 9, 2016 at Elim Church (419 Slimmon Rd). Arrangements in care of John Schachtel – MOURNING GLORY FUNERAL SERVICES 306-978-5200 mourningglory.ca